T0137727

FRESH EGGS

A Western Maryland Childhood

by

Alice Lorraine Faith

Order this book online at www.trafford.com
or email orders@trafford.com

Most Trafford titles are also available at major online book retailers.

Printed in the United States of America.

ISBN: 978-1-4269-5996-7 (sc)
ISBN: 978-1-4269-5995-0 (hc)
ISBN: 978-1-4269-5994-3 (e)

Library of Congress Control Number: 2011903458

Trafford rev. 03/03/2011

 www.trafford.com

North America & International
toll-free: 1 888 232 4444 (USA & Canada)
phone: 250 383 6864 ♦ fax: 812 355 4082

Alice

"You never outgrow the landscape of your childhood ... What's oldest in your memory you love best, cherish."

We Were the Mulvaneys
Joyce Carol Oates
1996

DEDICATION

I dedicate this book to my parents, Florence Vivian Davis and Lawrence Sherwood Faith, and to my older brother, Andrew Davis Faith. This book is also dedicated to the memory of my younger brothers, Gregory Oakes Faith and William Cass Faith, who both passed away in 1988. In our youth, we shared a very special relationship. I miss them so much.

ACKNOWLEDGMENTS

I thank my husband, David L. Trauger, who was kind enough to share our computer. He also edited the book and helped me find words for the more elusive ideas and memories emerging from the labyrinth of my brain. In addition to editing the book, my husband spent countless hours scanning and formatting the photographs --- a task more difficult than one might think! I also want to thank him for the comment, "I am so proud of you for doing this," that he occasionally repeated while I wrote and revised the manuscript over the past decade.

This book would not have been possible without the help of my kind, understanding, and very patient Mom, who passed away after I completed an earlier draft. While she was still alive, she answered dozens of questions that I had during the writing process. Although her memory was sometimes hazier than mine, she helped to provide or verify countless details and dates. Both of us wished that we had talked more with our Mothers earlier in our lives. Fortunately, writing this book gave me an opportunity to obtain information from Mom before it was too late.

I also appreciated the assistance of my brother Andy, my uncle, Robert (Bob) Davis, and my first cousin, Daniel (Danny) Davis, who was also a "partner in crime" during our youth, for helping me answer some additional questions.

Maxine Beachy Broadwater kindly granted permission to use a photograph of the National Hotel taken by her uncle, Leo Beachy.

Last, but not least, I want to thank Margie Burks, a former colleague of my husband's at Virginia Tech, for her help in editing this book. Although she grew up in California, our childhoods were similar in many ways, and reading this book brought back many youthful memories for her. Her perspective and assistance were greatly appreciated. Any remaining editorial issues are mine alone.

Alice L. Faith-Trauger

February 2011

PREFACE

*M*y name is Alice Lorraine Faith, at least, that was the name given to me at the time of my birth. I mention my original name because, over the years, I've had a few variations of my last name…but that's material for another book. I was born at approximately 9:30 a.m. on August 10, 1949, at the Hazel McGilvery Hospital in Meyersdale, Pennsylvania. I find it hard to believe that I was born so early in the morning, since I am definitely not a "morning person."

Meyersdale had the nearest hospital to my hometown, Grantsville, Maryland. The town of Meyersdale has not changed much over the years, but there have been some interesting changes since the time of my birth. The Hazel McGilvery Hospital no longer exists. This structure is now an apartment building. A new Meyersdale Community Hospital serves the region. The town also has acquired the nickname "Maple City" and the accompanying slogan, "The sweetest place on Earth."

I was named after the principal character in Lewis Carroll's "Alice in Wonderland" and for my maternal Grandmother (Lorraine). While writing this book, it became clear to me that being named after the "Alice" character in Carroll's book was appropriate. While growing up in Grantsville, which was my "wonderland," many things appeared larger than life to me. I was so small, and yet at other times, I felt like I was so big and important. And there were also some things that happened to me along the way that were kind of scary.

I wanted to write about my early childhood in Grantsville (1949-1963), because I believe that experiences during this period of my life had a profound impact on who I am today. Most people could make this statement, I suppose, but it was important for me to put down in writing my experiences growing up in this small town in western Maryland. Mostly, I wanted my son, Brendan Davis Pearson, to better know and understand his Mom, as well as to appreciate her family and small town roots.

This book is not intended to be a genealogical study. Therefore, I have not gone into depth about my ancestry. With my husband's help and experience in working with genealogy, I will continue to study the family roots of my Mother and Father. Perhaps this study will yield information for yet another book.

Several important notes: First, although this book concerns the years 1949 through 1963, occasionally, it was necessary to weave in experiences from later years of my life in order to complete or elaborate on a story. Second, I certainly have not remembered everything about my early childhood, and there may be some dates, events, things, or other details that have not been recalled as accurately as they should have been. However, I racked my brain to remember absolutely everything that I could in order to make this an interesting and accurate account of my young life. Third, in some instances, I felt that it was important not to reveal the names of certain individuals out of respect for living relatives.

I hope you enjoy this book. Although I occasionally had to type through torrents of tears, I, nevertheless, had great fun in writing it; the more I wrote, the more I remembered! Transferring the myriad of memories I have into written words to create this book has been a great catharsis and a sense of fulfillment for me. I now know myself much better!

Former Hazel McGilvery Hospital

CHAPTER 1

A "ONE LIGHT" TOWN

I grew up in Grantsville, a small rural community in western Maryland. The town was so small that there was only one traffic signal, constantly blinking its bright orange warning light at all travelers passing through the center of town. Grantsville is situated on U.S. Route 40, which over time has also been known as the National Highway, National Road, and National Pike.

This historic road originally began as Nemacolin's Path, a legendary Indian trail that traversed the dense virgin forests of this wilderness region. Nemacolin, a Delaware Indian Chief born 1715, guided frontiersmen in western Maryland. The old road's route closely followed the frontier trail originally surveyed by a 21-year-old George Washington in 1754 and later constructed by Major General Edward Braddock's British Army in 1755 during the French and Indian War.

Before he became our first President, George Washington foresaw the need for a road unifying the first states in the emerging new Nation. Writing in his diary in 1784, Washington expressed the need to "open a wide door, and make a smooth way for the Produce of the Country to pass to our markets." Although not many people settled in the rugged

Allegheny Mountains, they wanted access to the rich farmland in the region and beyond.

In order to make this happen, President Thomas Jefferson realized that more than an Indian path was needed for moving crops and goods from farms to marketplaces. Therefore, in 1806, President Jefferson asked Congress to appropriate the necessary money to build a trans-Appalachian land link, known as the "Cumberland Road." This road was the first highway built entirely with federal funds. Construction began in 1811 at Cumberland, Maryland. Later, the Cumberland Road became a toll road or turnpike known as the National Pike.

The National Pike connected with existing roads to Baltimore and was finished by 1818 as far as Wheeling, West Virginia. Eventually, the road extended through the Ohio River Valley, opening the Midwest for settlement and commerce. Thousands of settlers streamed by stagecoach and Conestoga wagon over the rugged Allegheny Mountains to the rich agricultural lands in Ohio, Indiana, and Illinois. Conestoga wagons, some brightly painted with red running gears, Prussian blue bodies, white canvas coverings, and pulled by teams of draft horses or oxen, were the most common vehicle for transporting heavy freight. They were considered the "tractor-trailer" of the 19th Century and averaged only 15 miles a day. The "speedy" stagecoach, however, averaged 60 to 70 miles in one day.

During its heyday, traffic was heavy both east and west over this mountain road. Grantsville was one of many small towns and villages along the road, where teamsters and travelers found accommodations and supplies. For several decades, the National Pike was the country's busiest artery to the heartland and became known as the "Main Street of America."

The National Pike served as a toll road under State control from 1835 to 1905. Visitors to western Maryland can still see white milepost markers and toll houses at various points along the road. This toll road, subsequently rebuilt as U.S. Route 40 and called the National Highway, connected with other highways so that a person could travel from coast to coast. When Interstate 68 was constructed between 1965 and 1991, its route paralleled Route 40, the former National Road, National Pike, Braddock's Trail, and Nemacolin's Path. Interstate 68 is called the National Freeway in homage to its historic predecessors.

Grantsville is located in Garrett County and is the incorporated town at the highest elevation along the National Pike in Maryland. Garrett County was separated from Allegany County in 1872 and was named in honor of John W. Garrett, who was, at that time, President of the Baltimore and Ohio Railroad. Garrett County is as far west as one can travel in Maryland before seeing the sign, "Welcome to Wild and Wonderful West Virginia." Grantsville is also near the Pennsylvania state border, just two miles south of the Mason-Dixon Line. In fact, walking to Springs, Pennsylvania, from Grantsville was an easy feat (pun intended) for those of us growing up there in the 1950's. I spent many warm spring and summer afternoons riding my small, trusty bicycle, with the big fat tires, back and forth across that State line.

Grantsville Landscape in Appalachian Mountains

Grantsville is a surprisingly old community. The origin of this small town was in 1785 when an Englishman named Daniel Grant, an engineer and innkeeper from Baltimore, bought land in western Maryland. However, it was not until ten years later, in 1796 that Daniel actually moved to his property located in northern Garrett County. He settled on one thousand acres in and around present day Grantsville. Daniel called his homestead "Cornucopia." He also named a small cluster of houses "Grant's Village" that evolved along the route constructed by General Braddock's troops during the French and Indian War. Grant's Village eventually became incorporated as Grantsville. Daniel Grant was considered the wealthiest person in the county at that time.

Oats and Corn

Western Maryland is an extraordinarily beautiful part of the United States. The rounded, undulating mountains with their panoramic vistas, are endowed with a wealth of natural resources that have created a number of important industries: mining, timbering, farming, and milling. However, my most vivid images of growing up in western Maryland are memories of farming: barns, farms, chickens, cows, and EGGS. In the 1950's, farming was the primary industry. In this region, the awe-inspiring, ancient Appalachian Mountains are dotted with fields growing a variety of crops: corn, alfalfa, and other small grains. Grantsville is considered "the heart" of some of the most productive farmland in the region.

Garrett County Farms

The gently rolling hills possess some lovely old farmhouses and barns and, of course, they are home to a variety of cows, chickens, and other barnyard animals that, in my mind, had personalities worthy of inclusion in George Orwell's "Animal Farm." However, most of these farms are not large, prosperous enterprises consisting of thousands of acres but rather many small farms that have been in families for generations. Many of the farms are owned and operated by either Amish or Mennonite families. There is a large population of both religious sects in western Maryland. The region surrounding Grantsville was then, and remains today, an economically depressed area. Eking out any kind of a living in this part of the country has not been easy in spite of the fertile land.

Grantsville used to be an exciting and vibrant place to live. At least it seemed that way to me. OK, exciting may be a stretch, but it was an interesting and fun place during my childhood.

When I was growing up in Grantsville, there were many small "Mom and Pop" businesses in town. I remember several grocery stores, Klotz Rexall drug store, a small five and dime-type variety store, Davis Hardware Store, Southern States Feed and Supplies, two insurance agencies: Harry C. Edwards and D. H. Hershberger, Beachy Lumber Company, Hagan Creamery, Flushing Shirt Manufacturing Company, Yoder's Locker Plant, three car dealerships: The Motor Service Company --- Ford, Grantsville Garage --- Dodge and Plymouth, and Casselman Motor Company --- Chevrolet, two in-home hair salons: Dot McCurdy's and Betty Jo Swauger's Beauty Lounge, a branch of the Ruth Enlow Library, Winterberg Funeral Home, two banks --- First State Bank and First National Bank, Grantsville Elementary School, at least two bars (and perhaps more bars than a child would be aware of), several churches and, believe it or not, three hotels: the Casselman, the National, and the Victoria. I know there were several other businesses in and around town, too. You would think that with all of these thriving endeavors, Grantsville would have had a population of over a thousand, but its inhabitants numbered well under this figure. Surprisingly, the population today is approximately 600, in spite of the fact that many of the above businesses are gone.

The small, locally owned, grocery stores in town are gone and probably long forgotten. They have been replaced by a large Foodland. Foodland is a nice store, but it does not hold a candle when it comes to the character and hometown warmth and charm of the smaller stores. I recall that one store located on the west end of town was called "Deffenbaugh's," another grocery store was "Huff's" located on the east side of town, and the store closest to where we lived, near the center of town, was "Herb Layman's" grocery store.

Because Mr. Layman's store was so convenient, I probably visited that store more often than the others. I remember Mr. Layman standing behind a counter at the far end of the long, narrow, dark store. He always had on a long white apron with what appeared to be blood stains on it; I hoped from butchering meat and stocking the display case! Mr. Layman was a tall, thin man who wore glasses and had straight, white, combed-back hair. He had a strong chin and he always appeared tanned, like he spent hours away from his store working outside in the sun. To me he seemed old.

As you entered Mr. Layman's store, the entire right side was a long, white cooler and freezer. It had a large slanted glass front so you could see all of the meats and assorted "cold" food items. To the left were shelves and shelves (almost to the ceiling) of canned and dry goods. Today, this unique old grocery store has been replaced by a liquor store.

I miss the small grocery stores in Grantsville. But what I miss the most of all of these former establishments is the grand old National Hotel, which stood for many years directly across from my Grandmother's house on Main Street. It broke my heart when they tore it down in 1984. I only ventured into this magnificent structure one time in 1982 to play a round of pool in the basement with my cousin Danny, but it was always a part of my young life and imagination. I wondered what the guest rooms looked like and what kind of people stayed there over its 157 years of history --- the stories those walls could tell! Today, in its place stands a gas station and mini-mart. I suppose tearing down the National Hotel was done in the name of "progress." But building a small, non-descript market, which sells potato chips, powdered donuts in a box, fingernail clippers, romance novels, and sandwiches to go, is not my idea of progress!

The National Hotel

I recall that there were many young families with small children and teenagers. The Grantsville Elementary School, where I spent many, many hours (grades 1 through 6) is now subdivided into apartments, several small businesses, including a large second-hand shop and antique vendor. A new elementary school was built nearby in the 1970's. All of the churches are in operation, but, the once active Catholic Church on Main Street has been converted into an antique shop. A new Catholic Church, St. Ann, is located just outside of the town limits.

The drug store holds special memories for me. I used to love to go there after school to get a "chocolate coca cola." Nearly everyday after school, every round, swiveling stool would be occupied. The kids would be talking loudly and laughing. I remember watching the owner, Frank Klotz behind the soda fountain leaning against the back counter with his white apron securely tied around his waist and his arms folded, watching all of the kids. He always wore a white or light-colored dress shirt with the sleeves rolled up to about mid-forearm. He responded immediately when another soda or milkshake was ordered. The food menu was standard fare for soda fountains --- hamburgers, French fries, and the like. Although I cannot recall how this food tasted, to young, hungry adolescents --- it was all delicious.

The one distinct personality trait that stands out in my memory about Frank Klotz was that he talked exceptionally fast and would often mumble his words. There were many times that I had absolutely no idea what he had said to me. A footnote about the drug store is that Frank Klotz's daughter-in-law turned the drug store into an antique shop called "Spinning Wheel and Dream Weavers Antiques." However, the antique shop closed a few years ago. Subsequently, the building was sold and a new business opened.

The drug store was also the place where Greg, Bill, and I would go to purchase a Mother's Day or Birthday gift for Mom. She would inevitably end up with a small, cobalt blue bottle of Evening in Paris perfume. This French perfume was touted as the fragrance used by more women than any other in the world in the 1950s. By 1969, however, it had vanished from American shelves. I vividly remember one special occasion. My younger brothers and I hurried down to the store to purchase a gift. We looked and looked. Finally we spotted it --- the perfect gift --- a powder compact for Mom. The square compact contained no face powder but, nonetheless, we thought it was stunning. It had a gold rim (not real gold of course) and it had red, black, and gold flecks embedded in the case. That was a real find for us!

One final, not so pleasant memory, that I have of the drug store involved a woman who used to come into the store from time to time. To a young girl, she seemed like a hideous monster. I will never forget how she looked. She would be dressed in dark, heavy clothing with long sleeves. She always wore a scarf to cover her head. All that one could really see was her face and hands, but that was enough. Her exposed skin was completely covered with large, ugly, protruding lumps. She was so deformed and horrible looking --- I could not stand to be near her or even to look at her. I never knew her name or anything about her. I suppose I didn't want to know anything. Mom remembered her, too, but she could not recall her name.

It was not until I reached adulthood and began thinking about my childhood, and specifically about this woman, that I realized that she may have had the same affliction as the "Elephant Man." That disease is called neurofibromatosis, but she had less severe symptoms. I watched the movie, which documented the life of Joseph Carey Merrick, the Englishman, who suffered from an extreme form of this tragic disease. I have since come to realize how devastated this woman must have been throughout her entire life. She was no doubt shunned by most people. Her desolate life must have been almost unbearable. How she managed the courage to walk into the drug store, I will never know. As an adult, I have overwhelming sadness and enormous sympathy for this woman. If I saw her today, I would say hello, and I would be more understanding and sympathetic.

I loved Grantsville then and I still enjoy visiting my hometown, but it certainly has changed. The town is very quiet now except for the occasional special event, such as "Grantsville Days." The predominant reason for the shift from a vibrant, interesting community to a rather sleepy, ordinary town is the fact that Interstate 68 bypassed Grantsville. Before this development, U.S. Route 40 ran straight through town down Main Street. The National Road was Grantsville's lifeblood for the town and the surrounding area. This prominent two-lane highway brought tourists and other travelers through our scenic area for decades. Today, people no longer have to drive through Grantsville on their journeys.

One fond memory I have is sitting on my Grandmother's enclosed, front porch on one of two massive rocking chairs. These old chairs were stuffed with horsehair and covered in dark brown leather. The chairs were so well used and worn that the leather was cracking, especially along the arms and in the seat of the chairs. If you weren't careful, you could get tiny, little scratches on your arms or legs from the damaged hide. Originally, they had belonged to Edmund and Lida Lomison, my maternal Great Grandparents.

My younger brothers and I would sit on the porch for hours peering out of the large windows which framed the south and east sides of the porch. The house faced south and was situated only yards away from Main Street and directly across from the historic National Hotel. This vantage point gave us a "bird's eye view" of the happenings in Grantsville. We would watch the many cars passing by Grandma's house and try to guess the color of the next one (it didn't take much to entertain us). Grandmother's front porch was my refuge. I always felt safe and happy there.

It is unfortunate that most tourists on their way to vacation at Deep Creek Lake or to distant points west now bypass Grantsville entirely. I don't think that peering out of front porch windows would be as much fun today. Although Grantsville is a small, quiet town, the area has some wonderful historic sites that should not be forgotten because of "progress."

The Casselman Bridge is Grantsville's most prominent landmark. It is a beautiful old stone bridge that was built in 1813. At that time, it was the largest single-span stone arch structure ever constructed in the world! At its "grand opening," the builder bravely and confidently stood under the bridge while its supporting timbers were being removed to prove wrong, the skeptics who said the bridge would collapse without support. Defying the naysayers, the bridge supported horse-drawn wagons, coaches, trucks, and automobiles for 140 years! Casselman Bridge was closed to traffic in 1953, when it was by-passed with Route 40 and a new bridge over the Casselman River was constructed. The Department of the Interior designated the iconic Casselman Bridge a Registered Historical Landmark.

Casselman Bridge

Another renowned site located in Grantsville is the Casselman Inn. It was first opened in 1824 and is still in operation today as both a hotel and restaurant. Over its many years of business, this hotel has been called Sterner's Tavern, Drover's Inn, Farmer's Hotel, and Dorsey's Hotel. It is interesting to note that Daniel Grant from whom Grantsville took its name was the original owner. The gentleman who built this historic hotel, Mr. Solomon Sterner, constructed it with bricks that were handmade on site. During the Civil War, the Casselman Inn became a makeshift hospital; generally for men wounded in the battles around Winchester, Virginia.

Casselman Inn

This impressive and beautiful old hotel is now the home of some lovely antique pieces of bedroom furniture that once furnished my Grandmother's house. Many years ago, my husband and I stopped at this establishment. I told them who I was and asked if I could see the room with my Grandmother's furniture. They took us up to the largest bedroom in this historic hotel. There was the high walnut bed and marble-top dresser that once graced my Grandmother's bedroom. Although this massive, ornate furniture was as beautiful as ever, it was even more beautiful in Grandmother's bedroom.

Grandma's Bed

Another notable landmark in Grantsville is Stanton's Mill, one of the oldest gristmills in Garrett County. Although the mill is now east of the heart of Grantsville, it was once the center of town. Jesse Tomlinson built the original mill in 1795. The mill was rebuilt in 1856 by Perry Schultz and deeded to William Stanton in 1862. Stanton's son, Eli, operated the mill for 43 years. This mill operated as an independent business until 1996, when the Spruce Forest Artisan Village group purchased it. Up to that time, it was the oldest, continuous operating business in western Maryland. Several years ago Stanton's Mill reopened as an operating mill. In keeping with the mill's historic past, they grind wheat and grains between large mill stones that grind at lower temperatures than modern milling methods. It is believed that this grinding method yields products of superior taste, texture, and nutritional value. They use no chemicals or preservatives. The mill produces graham, whole wheat, seven grain, rye, buckwheat, and white unbleached flours. They also make yellow and white corn meal and grits, corn muffin mix, hush puppy mix, buckwheat pancake mix and Amish funnel cake mix.

Grantsville is also the home of Penn Alps. This large log building was built as a stagecoach stop on the National Pike in 1818, and was originally called the "Little Crossings Inn." Penn Alps was remodeled and now serves as a popular restaurant and souvenir shop. Adjacent to Penn Alps are relocated and restored log cabins, schoolhouses, and other rustic structures --- some dating back to the pre-Revolutionary War era. These historic buildings are now home to a thriving craft industry and are a key tourist attraction in the area.

During my youth, I had no idea of the historic significance of this locale and the role this community played in opening the western frontier to settlement. It was only later when I was working with others in the community to develop the Grantsville Community Museum that I learned about people, places, and events occurring here over the past 250 years. For example, George Washington's surveys along Nemacolin's path, General Braddock's encampment at Little Crossing during the French and Indian War, history of the National Pike, photography of Leo Beachy, and crash of the B-52 bomber in 1964 are but a few of the interesting and unique local happenings. This knowledge contributed to a deeper understanding of my roots and the community that shaped my childhood and personality.

CHAPTER 2

LORRAINE AND NORMAN

*M*y maternal Grandparents, Estella Lorraine Davis, nee Lomison and Norman Robert Davis, both grew up in Allenwood, Union County, Pennsylvania. Allenwood, located in the central part of the state, is approximately 170 miles "as the crow flies" northeast of Grantsville. The Davis and Lomison family homes were adjacent to the majestic, tranquil, and beautiful Susquehanna River.

Norman   **Lorraine**

Davis Wedding Photos

On June 7, 1912, Lorraine (Grandma never liked her first name and always used Lorraine) and Norman were married in Allenwood. They were married by Norman's Father, Lewis Cass Davis, who was a Baptist Minister. Lorraine and Norman had likely known each other since their youth. They had two children: Florence Vivian Davis born October 24, 1920; and Norman Robert Davis Jr. born May 30, 1924. In their day, the Davis' were a couple that one would likely refer to in today's vernacular as "the beautiful people." My Grandmother was a lovely woman; my Grandfather was a handsome man.

Grandfather was born on June 9, 1888; he died from pancreatic cancer on February 11, 1952. His parents were Lewis Cass Davis and Mary Emma Purdy Davis, both of Allenwood, Pennsylvania. Grandfather had two brothers, Malcolm and Earl, and two sisters, Ruth and Darle. I never knew Grandfather's brothers or sisters, but growing up, I was told stories about Malcolm and Darle. Earl Davis was killed in 1903 when he was 17 years old in a munitions plant explosion at Elmira, New York. No pictures exist of him. He is buried in Allenwood, according to Uncle Bob.

My cousin Danny actually knew Great Aunt Darle. When Danny was 16, he and a friend, Gerald Beachy, traveled to England to work on a farm owned by the Beachy family. Danny stayed on the farm for 2 months. While there, he managed to contact Darle Davis, who was living in Cheltenham, England. They arranged to meet at the train station, but they missed each other because neither one knew what the other one looked like. They likely passed each other a dozen times in the station. This mix-up continued for nearly two hours, but neither one of them thought to use the station's public address system to facilitate contact. In frustration and disappointment, Danny returned to the farm, where he called Darle again. They decided that Danny would take a taxi to her flat in Cheltenham, because the bus trip would take more than 4 hours one way. So, eventually they connected.

Initially, Danny only intended to visit Darle for a day, but he ended up staying with her for a week. Darle took him sightseeing all over the countryside, including to Shakespeare's birthplace, Stratford-on-Avon. She even let Danny drive the car. What a treat for him and an adventure driving on the left side of the road! As Danny explained to me, Darle was a Doctor of Radiology, but she appeared to be rather poor. She lived in a small apartment, which Danny said looked like it must have been her office at one time. All sorts of medical equipment were installed in her flat. She had no refrigerator and lived a rather meager existence. But, she had a little car and she sure got around. Darle never married.

There was one possible reason for Darle's apparent lack of money. According to Mom, Darle had written a letter to Grandma explaining that one of Malcolm's sons had invested her money and for some reason the investment failed. Darle lost nearly all of her money. I do not have any specifics about this investment scheme but this could account to some degree for Darle's living situation. She died and is buried somewhere in London, England.

Malcolm lived and worked in Rochester, New York. He was a mechanical engineer and his occupation was listed in the Rochester City Directory as a "Designer." He was employed for many years by the Eastman-Kodak Company. I have been told that he knew Albert Einstein. Malcolm once asked Einstein if he would like to go fishing in Canada with him, and he accepted! Malcolm also wrote and published a book about physics entitled simply: "Relativity." If Malcolm and

Einstein were indeed friends, they no doubt had much in common. Malcolm Purdy Davis' book was published May 25, 1943. If one was interested, a copy could be found in the Library of Congress. One noteworthy comment: shortly after the book's publication, the University of Utah Physics Department requested a large number of Malcolm's book to be used as a reference for physics classes taught there. Malcolm also had a variety of hobbies, and he was a very talented painter. He had a power boat and enjoyed taking it out on the lake. He also built a radio!

Malcolm was married three times. His first wife, Martha Irwin, was stricken with bone cancer when she was pregnant with her only child. Martha refused to abort the fetus and, as a result, her leg had to be amputated. She died at the age of 23 years, 1 month, on August 5, 1910; only a few months after giving birth to a son they named Harry. Malcolm arranged to have his son stay with aunts for two years. A close family member revealed that Malcolm, understandably, became quite depressed after the death of Martha and that this may have contributed to a strained relationship between Malcolm and Harry.

Eventually, Malcolm reunited with Harry when he married his second wife, Georgia Salmon. They had three children, Charles, Ethel, and Thelma. Georgia died in 1929 at the age of 39, when her children were relatively young. Subsequently, Malcolm married Augusta "Gussie" Lemcke. They had no children. Malcolm, age 70, died in 1950 and Gussie, age 59, died in 1954. Malcolm's children are all deceased. Harry had several children, Charles had two daughters, Ethel had one daughter, and Thelma never married. Malcolm, Georgia, and Augusta are buried along with Thelma in a Davis family plot in the Riverside

Cemetery, in Rochester, New York. Martha is buried with other Davis'
in Allenwood, Pennsylvania.

Great Catch: Malcolm and Grandfather

Like Malcolm, Grandfather was an avid fisherman. He usually went
to Canada for his fishing trips. He also liked to hunt, but apparently
fishing was his great passion. Although I do not remember any mounted
fish in Grandma's house, there were several mounted hunting trophies
including an osprey, a deer head, and a bobcat (although there seems to
be some question as to who shot the bobcat). In addition to fishing and
hunting, Grandfather was a pretty good tennis player --- good enough
to be in competition.

Grandfather resided in Allenwood until he began his education at
nearby Bucknell Academy (now Bucknell University) at Lewisburg,
Pennsylvania. He attended Bucknell in the early 1900's, and then
enrolled at the University of Pennsylvania in Philadelphia, where
he received his pre-medical degree. He then attended the Maryland
Medical College of Baltimore, where he received his medical degree on

May 26, 1913. After completing his medical internship, Grandfather and his new bride moved to Henry, West Virginia, where he practiced medicine for a coal company located near this small town.

On May 2, 1917, Grandfather enlisted in the U.S. Army. Called for service on August 9th, he was commissioned as a First Lieutenant, and subsequently was promoted to the rank of Captain. Grandfather sailed overseas from New York on the 12th of September, 1917, and landed in Liverpool, England. He served as a surgeon in the 19th Battalion, Duke of Wellington's West Riding Regiment, with the 69th Infantry Brigade, 23rd (British) Division in Italy during World War I.

Grandfather, front and center, and Medical Corps

I wish that my Grandfather were still with us so that I could talk to him about his experiences during this defining moment in America's history. Mom told me one surprising and humorous story. Apparently a dance was held in honor of the American soldiers stationed in

England. Among those soldiers in attendance was my Grandfather. Because very few, if any, women attended this dance, the men danced with each other. It so happened, that Edward VIII, the Prince of Wales, was also in attendance, and he danced with my Grandfather. What a remarkable story! I wish I had a picture of that once-in-lifetime event. Prince Edward later became the King of England, but shortly thereafter, abdicated the throne to marry Mrs. Wallis Simpson.

Grandfather: A Dashing Military Man

Grandfather was awarded several medals for his military service. Prominent among them was the bestowment of the British Bronze Medal for Valor for military operations in Italy during October 26-27, 1918. Lieutenant Norman Robert Davis was the Battalion Medical Officer. The citation accompanying the Bronze Medal states that he "showed the utmost gallantry and disregard for personal danger in carrying out his duties of attending the wounded. On one occasion, his Aid Post was being very heavily shelled. Lieut. Davis at extreme personal risk remained at his post…rather than move to a safer place for fear of missing any wounded being brought back. His gallant conduct during the whole operation was most noticeable."

Grandfather was also awarded the Italian Bronze Medal from the Commander-in-Chief of The Italian Forces on January 11, 1919. On April 16, 1919, he sailed from Brest, France, and landed in New York 10 days later. He received his honorable discharge at Camp Dix, New Jersey on April 29, 1919. There, he received the World War I Victory Medal. After World War II, U.S. veterans of World Wars I and II, who were decorated while serving with Allied forces, were awarded the equivalent U.S. decorations; Grandfather received the Silver Star at that time.

After military service, Grandfather returned to Henry, West Virginia, where he resumed his medical practice with the coal company. Apparently, Grandfather had been away so long that he and Grandmother felt like "strangers" upon his return. They must have overcome this initial awkwardness, however, because Mom was born the following year in Henry. Sadly, the mining town of Henry, West Virginia, no longer exists --- another victim of progress.

In late 1920, my Grandparents moved to Grantsville, Maryland, where they remained throughout the rest of their lives. My Grandfather practiced general medicine in Grantsville until the time of his death in 1952. His doctor's office was located in the front part of his large house on Main Street.

One of Mom's early memories was of her Father and his friend (Bert Swauger) hooking up two of Grandfather's three horses to a sleigh on snowy, cold days (sometimes in the middle of the night) in order to visit patients. He called many of these visits "confinement" cases. This is an outdated medical term, but apparently it referred to women who were pregnant.

While going through boxes of old photographs, cards, and letters in my Mom's house, I stumbled upon a folded up letter and two yellowed newspaper articles pertaining to an incident that took place in July of 1933. After a five-day investigation, a man was arrested on a charge of attempting to extort $1,000 from my Grandfather. This man was a 60-year-old farmer who lived in the area. A thousand dollars was an extraordinary amount of money to a poor farmer in 1933. The investigation began after Grandfather received a letter demanding that money be placed under the steps of the Reformed Church at New Germany, near the perpetrator's farm. The following is a transcription of the letter sent by this man in its entirety and verbatim.

Dr. Davis – Sir, we are taking this plan to help the neady poor people and save homes by making loans in this way, you have been choosen for one to make a loan of a thousand dollars to pay back to another party that made a loan

You will get your money back with intrest. In $5-10-20 nothing biger than $20 bills. Wrap in a package good take it out and put under the steps safe going in the front way at the Reform Church at New Germany which is the one below as you come to the churches, we choose this place to be safe have it there by Thursday night the 27th of July between Eleven and twelve oclock have no one with you nor anyone to watch the place. You are not to show this letter to anyone tell no one what you want the money for. This is strictly confidential, if you cause no trouble & obey these orders you will not be harmed in any way the C-C will protect you.

If you fail to obey these orders first your property will be blowed up second you or some of your family will be Kid Naped & third you will be burnt at the stake, so follow out all we ask by making us this loan of a thousand dollars, it is for a good cause & keep people from lousing their homes. This means the money or your life which will be done, we don't want trouble unless we have to. Keep your head shut and make no trouble in anyway.

Remember the time and date 27th July you know the Banks have all the money tied up, then how is people to live or pay a debt this is one way to help. Do your best this way. Ordered by Clu Clan Comity.

As a result of handwriting analysis, additional evidence, and this person's confession to sending the letter, an arrest was made. All materials and facts relating to the case were turned over to Federal authorities. There is no explanation in the newspaper articles as to what eventually happened to the farmer. When this happened, Grandfather was not only the town Doctor, but he also served as President of the First State Bank in Grantsville. There is little wonder why he was targeted for this crime.

I have no early memories of my Grandfather, as I was only three years old when he passed away. By all accounts, he must have been an extraordinary individual. Years later, several people that I met in Grantsville related stories to me about their experiences with "Dr. Davis" or mentioned that they were delivered by him. I am sorry I never knew him.

My Grandma was born on August 3, 1885, and died from congestive heart failure on May 29, 1973. Her parents were Edmund Lee Lomison and Lida Fisher Lomison, both of Allenwood, Pennsylvania. She had one sister, Edith Lomison. Grandma attended business college and then worked briefly with the railroad. Grandma's mother, Lida, lived with my Grandparents for nine years after the death of her husband, Edmund. Lida died of a heart attack in September 1943 at the age of 86. In a local newspaper, obituary notice, one quote stands out: "She had a very quiet and pleasing personality and will be greatly missed by her family and friends."

Unlike my Grandfather, I knew my Grandma rather well. She lived right next door to us in Grantsville, and I spent many happy hours with her. I loved her and I thought she was a remarkable woman.

My Grandma was a tall woman. When I knew her, she was also rather heavy set. She always wore her curled hair up in a very fine hairnet. It was as if she had a delicate cobweb covering her hair. After Grandma washed her hair in the kitchen sink, Mom would help her set it. This task was accomplished with "hundreds" of skinny bobbie pins holding just as many tiny curls close to her head. Grandma often walked around in her bare feet, and I remember thinking that she seemed to have extraordinarily long ears. She rarely wore jewelry. She needed eyeglasses but her twinkly blue eyes could not be missed. Her attire was usually a short-sleeved, flowery cotton dress. Although I never knew her to wear slacks, I suspect she may have worn the "pants" in the family. She loved to sit in her favorite chair in the evening and watch "The Lawrence Welk Show." I often watched this program with her. Grandma also adored peach ice cream (you could always find a gallon of it in her freezer), and she would sometimes consume a large bowl of it while watching television.

I consider Grandma to be a renaissance woman. She was ahead of her time in many ways. She not only attended business school, but she worked outside of the home in the early 1900's. She occasionally assisted my Grandfather with his medical practice by welcoming patients into the waiting room area. After Grandfather passed away, she helped her son, Robert, with bookkeeping duties required to operate the Davis Hardware Store.

Grandma's Oil Paintings

Most notably, Grandma was a prolific oil painter for many years. She painted a myriad of scenic landscapes --- covered bridges, country barns, majestic mountains, and beautiful sunsets, just to name a few. Mom possessed many of her paintings. Grandma did not start to paint with gusto until she was much older --- reminiscent of Grandma Moses. She used to "practice" to get the color and the consistency of the oil paint just right on a large, bulbous-shaped gourd. As far as I know, she never painted human figures, but she did paint tiny angels, leaves, dots, etc., on this gourd that remind me of Grandma Moses' "primitive" style of artwork. On the bottom of the gourd, she printed in red paint the words, "1959 Grantsville Garden." I have this wonderful folk art heirloom in my home today.

My older brother, Andy was instrumental in helping my Grandma with her masterpieces. I am not sure whose responsibility it was to find the images, but scenic pictures were cut out of magazines like National Geographic and Life. Andy would then lightly sketch the scenes onto the canvas with a pencil as a blueprint for Grandma's paintings. She always sat either in her kitchen in front of a north-facing window, or on her back porch when painting at her easel. She said that natural sunlight was the best lighting possible for painting. On one occasion, Grandma was invited to display her artwork in Oakland, the Garrett County seat. This event created considerable interest in her paintings; however, she made it clear that they were "Not For Sale!" Andy and I now have Grandma's paintings hanging throughout our homes.

My Grandma was also an avid rock and crystal collector. She had hundreds of different kinds of minerals in her collection all categorized and labeled. They were kept in specially designed upright gray cabinets, with skinny trays that slid in and out and divided into many tiny, cubbyholes. She had drawers and drawers full of a great variety of specimens. Andy also helped Grandma with this interesting hobby, and he maintains this collection in his home today.

In addition to the rock collection, Grandma had a large assortment of tea cups and saucers of fine bone china. They were neatly showcased along the long, white, built-in shelves that lined the walls of the first floor bathroom. They were beautiful to behold --- delicate and intricately decorated with floral designs of all sizes, shapes, and colors. The handles on many of these cups were so small that one could not even get a finger into the opening to hold onto it.

Grandma had another unusual and truly startling collection, which was stored in cupboards below the teacups. (I neglected to say that this was an unusually large bathroom.) She had stacks and stacks of Playboy magazines, dating back to some of the very earliest issues.

I discovered this collection one day and did my eyes ever get big. I have often wondered who the "collector" really was. If indeed it was Grandma, why? Grandma loved the human form. I think that this adoration comes naturally with many artistic individuals, especially painters. However, she never painted nudes. Oh well, she probably subscribed to Playboy so that she could read the articles. As I said, Grandma was ahead of her time.

Grandma was a great cook --- at least I thought that she was. She concocted all kinds of delectable dishes in the kitchen. She made the best pancakes, so big that they filled the old, black, cast iron, frying pan in which she cooked them. No silver dollar-sized pancakes in that kitchen! She also made wonderful tapioca, baked beans, and pies. Grandma used to bake lemon meringue pies and set them on the back porch to cool. Enormous, shiny golden beads of sugar would form on their fluffy, white surfaces. They were so tasty. Because of her pies, lemon meringue is one of my favorite choices for dessert. She also produced some of the best pumpkin pies I have ever eaten. To this day, they remain one of my favorite after dinner delights; I have been known to eat cold pumpkin pie for breakfast!

Grandma also cooked the tastiest green beans. We would pick them from our garden and then snap hundreds of long, thin, lumpy beans into a large, dented, aluminum cooking pot. They would be cooked with pieces of bacon and potato, and served in a little side dish with a splash of vinegar poured over them --- I can still smell them.

My Grandma was such a talented and interesting individual. I wish that she were still alive, so that I could talk with her. I am a different person now and I know that I could learn a great deal from her. Yes, she had another side to her just as we all do. According to Mom, she could be stubborn, ornery, and manipulative at times. Apparently, she was also a formidable woman. I learned many years later that some townspeople were afraid of her. Nevertheless, Grandma was a remarkable and unique human being. I miss her.

A Great Happy Grandma, February 1962
Written on back of photo:
"I had no idea I looked like this, Lorraine"

CHAPTER 3

GRANDMA'S BIG GREEN HOUSE

*G*randma's house seemed enormous to me --- as big as an English castle. A hedge, as tall as a Baltimore skyscraper and as thick as the Black Forest, surrounded the entire east side of the house and a portion of the front or south side. For shortcuts, my brothers, Cousin Danny, and I used to crawl back and forth through that hedge, creating a gaping hole in this beautiful living wall. This would make my Grandmother absolutely furious! "You kids stop that right now!" She uttered that phrase a lot. Another favorite saying of my Grandmother was: "It just gives me balls in my stomach." I am certain that we gave her plenty of balls in her stomach!

1956	**Today**

Grandma's House

The house also had an added buffer of privacy, in that four enormous maple trees stood proudly next to the sidewalk in front of the house. Sadly, the beautiful, old trees are gone now. Back then, Grandma's house was a vibrant shade of green. Not the washed out pale green it is today, but as green as a healthy, fat frog!

The house had five bedrooms --- four of them were large but one was long, narrow, and rather small. Throughout our childhood, Andy lived next door to us in my Grandmother's house; his was the long narrow bedroom. Consequently, Andy and I essentially lived in separate households. We were six years apart in age, so I was not as close to him as I was to my two younger brothers. Each of the large bedrooms was full of mammoth, dark, ornately and beautifully carved furniture. Andy's room, however, was cozy, functional, and basic --- lots of books, a roll top desk, a chest of drawers, a beloved stamp collection, a clothes closet, and a single bed.

In order to get to one of the inner bedrooms, you had to walk through an outer bedroom. This inner bedroom was secluded from the rest of the house and was my Mom's bedroom when she was a little girl. The hidden bedroom also concealed a surprise. It had a secret passageway, which lead to the bedroom where my Grandfather slept. To a small child, this was an astonishing discovery. I loved walking back and forth through this dark, mysterious passageway even though I had to make my way through a gauntlet of old clothes, shoes, and other dusty stuff.

Grandma's house was chock full of antiques. There were old mantel clocks, bentwood and platform rockers, an assortment of chairs, tables, lamps, and benches (including a deacon's bench), large oak bookcases with glass doors, old oil paintings, and two pianos. Grandma occasionally played the vertical piano located in the "game" room. The other large, flat piano was used only as an expensive resting place for lamps, books, assorted knick knacks, and anything else needing a special resting "spot." There were countless old tools in the basement, seasoned toys and vintage clothes in the attic, as well as priceless pottery and antiquated books nearly everywhere in the house. Sadly, many of these lovely things were sold at the 1982 auction ten years after her death.

One of the marvelous things about Grandma was that she managed to label just about every little knick-knack, gadget, and piece of jewelry in the house. The label would usually include the year in which she received it and the name of the person who gave it to her. I have one old pitcher of hers on the bottom of which is a tiny, yellowed piece of paper with the simple typed message: "1912. L. Davis." On one piece of jewelry that I inherited, there is an accompanying tag with the handwritten message: "Xmas 1909, Edith Lomison, From Dad, when she went in training." Edith Lomison was Grandma's younger sister and she trained to become a registered nurse at the Jefferson Hospital in Philadelphia, Pennsylvania. Another small piece of jewelry is labeled: "This is my sister Edith's nursing pin Jefferson Hospital 1910." On another very small pin, Grandma wrote on one side of the tag: "This is very old Annie B. Moore gave it to me." On the other side of the tag it reads: "Heirloom do not wear it." It is unfortunate, but in today's hectic and sometimes apathetic world, I believe very few individuals take the time or have the inclination to perform such a thoughtful gesture for posterity as to identify their most personal possessions.

Another endearing habit that Grandma had was writing specific instructions and securing them over various sinks, hot water radiators, and other appliances throughout the house. These notes were usually handwritten in red ink on 5" by 8" or smaller pieces of paper. They gave the user precise directions on how to turn something on or off, which way to turn it, and to please make sure that whatever you just did was done correctly! Because these instructions were around wet, steamy, or humid places, the red ink was usually smudged and the paper was yellowed with time. I am sure that those instructions had been read hundreds of times over the years.

As a little girl this big, old house often frightened me. Certain areas of the house always seemed to be extraordinarily dark and shadowy. The high ceilings, dark-stained wood, massive pieces of furniture, dark thick carpeting, and heavy draperies, only added to this "House of Usher" environment. I would often find myself in the house and it "seemed" like I was alone. It would be deathly quiet but I could always hear the far away ticking of a clock. I would walk very slowly at first, looking all about me to make sure that I was indeed alone. My eyes remained so wide open without blinking, for so long, that one would think that they had been frozen open. My heart raced and I couldn't wait to get close enough to a front or back door to make a sudden and hasty retreat.

I vividly remember one night I decided to spend the night at Grandma's. I was so excited. I got all ready for bed. I was going to sleep outside of the "secluded" bedroom, directly across the hall from Andy's bedroom. Only Grandma and I were there at the time. Andy must have been away. Grandma decided that we needed a snack before we retired. She opened the refrigerator door, pulled out two bananas and handed one to me. She always kept bananas in the refrigerator; it turned their yellow skins absolutely black but the cold kept their sweet, white "innards" perfect. I ate my banana and ascended the long staircase to the bedroom.

I do not remember what time it was, but I don't think I went to sleep at all that night. For some reason, I became paralyzed with fear. I lay sleepless underneath the covers for what seemed like an eternity. Somehow I managed to get up enough courage to jump out of bed, run down the stairs, and out of the house into the pitch black night. I raced across the cold, wet lawn in my bare feet, through our back door, onto the back porch, through the kitchen and living room and up the stairs to my bed. Thank goodness all of the doors were unlocked! Another lost benefit of small town, country living, unthinkable in today's world.

On another evening, years later after Grandma had passed away, a friend and I decided to stay in the house overnight. (I am only discussing this later period in my life to point out the fear continued to "haunt" me even in later years). My friend and I were definitely alone in the house. We had gotten ready for bed and were already snuggled in for the evening. We were in the bedroom where my Grandfather slept. It was eerily quiet.

We had noticed earlier what seemed to be a very strange phenomenon. Along the hallway on the second floor of Grandma's house, two, large, dark oil paintings hung on the wall across from Grandfather's bedroom. These portraits were painted by my Great Grandfather, Lewis Cass Davis, of himself and his wife, Emma Purdy Davis. The dark eyes of the images appeared to follow us wherever we went. Consequently, we were "spooked" before we even went to bed! The more we gazed across the room to these portraits, the more we got ourselves worked up. Finally, to stay another minute in that house became impossible. We jumped out of bed, got dressed, ran to the car, and drove to the nearest motel. We returned the next morning when everything appeared safe in the light of day.

There is a colorful story, not necessarily true, behind those two oil paintings. I was told that the hole evident in one of the paintings was a "bullet hole!" Apparently, my ancestors often had raging debates about stories in the Bible. According to family lore, one evening my relatives were discussing Noah's Ark --- something about getting all of those animals on board. One of them got so angry that they shot or threw something, and the flying missile hit the painting. It sounds to me like that hole could have very easily been a bullet hole considering all of those heated religious arguments!

Later, these paintings hung in Mom's bedroom in Catonsville. From time to time, these images may have been confidants for Mom. I am certain that her thoughts, ideas, and feelings were shared with these old paintings, never to be heard or known to the outside world. And, most importantly, the paintings could not talk back!

Grandma's house had many rooms besides the second floor bedrooms. The house faced south. The first floor rooms were sandwiched between large, long front and back porches. Adjacent to the front porch, was a rather small room which once served as Grandfather's examining room. It had long since been converted into a space for Grandma's extensive rock and crystal collection.

Just behind Grandfather's former examining room was another room, which I remember as the "game" room, but one might consider it a parlor. This is where Grandma and several of her friends played bridge at the card table, and where she sometimes played the upright or vertical piano. This piano was Grandmother's wedding gift from Grandfather in 1912. [Note: In 2010, this piano found its way back into our family; my brother Andy has restored it.] The grandchildren also played board games in this room. One game, which we would play for hours, was called "Carrom."

Grandma's Vertical Piano

Carrom was played on a square, wooden board, which covered the entire top of a card table. Players would flick a hard, round, wooden piece of a certain color with a finger and try to hit the other pieces of the same color into side pockets made of netting. It was similar to the game of pool only fingers were used instead of cue sticks. As in pool, the game piece which you were flicking could not go into the side pocket, only the piece which was being hit could disappear from the table. The person getting the most pieces into the side pockets would be the winner. The winner would usually be the player with the sorest finger, too!

The two porches were heavily used, especially during the spring and summer months. Besides the two old, dark brown leather rocking chairs, the front porch was furnished with two bentwood rockers and a wide, platform, glider swing. The fabric covering the swing was awning material with colorful orange and green stripes. I think that there was even fringe hanging somewhere off of it. The swing had a long green plastic pad that covered the entire seat, and it made a very distinctive "springy" noise during its back and forth movements. The front porch was where we would sit or swing or rock while we were watching the rain falling or the cars and the people passing by. The porch also afforded a great vantage point to observe the activity around the National Hotel. I loved the front porch; it was my favorite part of the house.

One final detail about the front porch was the floor covering. Centered on top of a large portion of the wooden floor was a straw-like, hard mat that was about one-half inch in thickness. The intricate design of the mat created many grooves and openings --- you could see the floor through the mat. If one stood on this mat for very long in bare feet (we were always barefoot), the skin on the bottom of your feet (especially your heels) would begin to sink into these tiny crevices causing the bottoms of your feet to hurt. Also the bottoms of your feet would look just like the pattern in the mat.

The back porch was important also, at least to me, because that is where all of those wonderful, just-out-of-the-oven pies were set out to cool. The back porch, like the front porch, had large picture windows that faced to the north and to the west. Needless to say, the back porch was an ideal vantage point for Grandma to keep an ever-watchful eye over her grandchildren, who were playing in the backyard. The living room was one long, rectangular area but it was divided into two specific areas by the use of heavy, black and gold, brocade draperies tied back in the middle and held securely with gold tasseled ropes. A straight valance hung from the ceiling, adding to the separation and the illusion that there were two rooms. Each portion of this room was furnished as distinct rooms with a couch, one or two large chairs, and assorted lamps, paintings, and tables.

It is in one of these sections (the one closest to the kitchen and the one which housed the large, flat, unplayed piano) that Grandma spent many hours sitting in her favorite chair watching television. It is rather humorous that the large console television was situated in one section of the living room just beyond the heavy draperies, and Grandma chose to sit in the other section. It always seemed like she was sitting so far away from the set. Besides watching television, she sometimes entertained in this area of the house, but mostly it served as a passageway from the front of the house to the kitchen.

There was a rather large, dark room just behind the back porch. I don't remember a light ever being turned on in this portion of the house. This room, at least while I was growing up was never used; it simply "housed" a large dining room table, a long buffet table with drawers, and several other pieces of furniture. On top of the buffet table was a wooden box in which beautiful, old, ornate silverware was kept. I also remember a large, gray, mounted osprey with wings spread wide and perched on top of this table. This bird was purchased by next-door neighbors at the estate auction after Grandma died. There were several other pieces of furniture. I suspect that this room was originally intended to be the dining room.

There was a long hallway that ran parallel with the staircase leading to the second floor and extended from the front of the house to the dining room and back porch. The one memorable thing about this hallway was that this was where the mounted, stuffed bobcat had his permanent home on top of a glass-fronted, oak bookcase! Mom did not know the full story behind the mounted bobcat. She remembered being told that Grandpa had shot it, but she had her doubts. We found a picture in an old family album and at first we thought it was her father holding the cat, but Mom noticed that it was not him. We don't know whether Grandfather shot it and then had a friend hold it up for the camera, or if the friend shot the animal.

This bobcat always fascinated me. His yellowed teeth were bared and his bristly, pink tongue was arched as was his back. He always looked to me as if he could pounce on the next unsuspecting person to pass by the bookcase.

The second most important room in the house, besides the front porch, was the kitchen. In contrast to the other ornately decorated rooms of the house, the kitchen was quite austere. There was a plain, white refrigerator, a dining table (rarely used for dining, but rather as an additional surface for putting "stuff"), a white gas stove, a sink, a china cabinet with glass doors installed over a tall, hot-water radiator, and a large storage cabinet attached to the opposite wall. This cabinet, used for storing canned goods and other staples, was constructed over a tin-topped storage cabinet attached to the floor. The cabinet had enough surface area on top, that Grandma could roll out her pie dough and do her canning. Both the china cabinet and the storage cabinets were painted a dark, chocolate brown. I don't know what kind of wood was beneath the paint.

Finally, there was a rather plain, wide, rectangular-shaped bench covered with a cream-colored oilcloth. Mom wished that she had kept this particular piece of furniture for reasons only known to her. Perhaps she had some special childhood memories. This bench was situated between the food storage cupboards and the kitchen sink and in front of an east-facing window. This is the place where we would snap green beans or sit and talk to Grandma while she was cooking or puttering around in the kitchen. The kitchen was always light and airy and was also one of the rooms in the house where Grandma painted. I have nothing but good memories of Grandma's kitchen.

I must tell you about the east-facing window in Grandma's kitchen. Uncle Bob and Aunt Jane had a Boston terrier named "Pat." Several times a day they let Pat out for his daily constitutions. Occasionally, I watched Pat. Upon his exit out of the front door, he would quickly run down a long flight of stairs (Bob and Jane lived in the apartment above the store next door) and then bolt across our front lawn and into his little assigned pen. Pat was so well trained. He did his "business" right under Grandma's kitchen window and nowhere else! He would then run out of the pen right through Grandma's hedge sometimes, bounce around in our front yard a few times, and then bound up the stairs. Oh well, he was a cute dog. He was a little black and white dog with large, bulgy brown eyes.

The basement was a part of the house of which I had great trepidation. It was so very dark, dank, and musty smelling down there. Part of this distinct smell came from the small storage cellar where Grandma kept such items as potatoes and bushels of apples. At the top of the stairs you had to pull on a long string attached to a single, bare light bulb before descending to the "dungeon." I was certain that something, or someone, lived down there that had not been invited.

I also worried that somehow I would become ensnared in the old, white wringer machine that Grandma had in the basement. This old piece of equipment, worthy of placement in a Smithsonian museum, was used to remove excess water from wet clothes fresh from the washing machine. The clothes were then ready to be hung outside on a line for drying. Wet clothes were fed through two fast moving, opposing rollers, and they would be so mashed down and stiff upon their exit, that you could lean the still damp clothes up against a wall! I sometimes wondered what I would look like if my entire body went through this process. The saying, "I've been through the wringer" certainly has real meaning for me. Thankfully, I spent as little time as possible in the basement!

The huge attic of Grandma's house was also a rather eerie place. To reach this portion of the house, you had to pull on a cord hanging from the ceiling that would lower a set of stairs. I would go up to the attic from time to time; I'm not sure why --- I think just to snoop around. Grandma's dark and dusty attic remained the same over the years, chockfull of old trunks, furniture and boxes. But the one thing which I will always remember about the attic was that I was sure that at some point during my wanderings over the dark, creaky, floorboards, I would fall through and land, hopefully alive, somewhere on a lower level of the house.

Grandma's house holds so many childhood memories for me. Sometimes, in dreams or even when I am fully awake, I will travel through the house in my mind's eye and see nearly everything as it was --- even Grandma sitting in her favorite chair in one corner of the living room near a window and next to the piano.

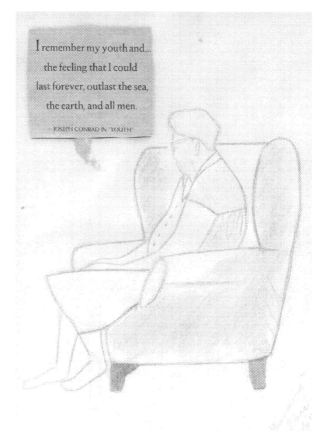

I remember my youth and...
the feeling that I could
last forever, outlast the sea,
the earth, and all men.

JOSEPH CONRAD IN "YOUTH"

My Pencil Sketch of Grandma

My Mom and Dad kept the house in the family for ten years after Grandma's death in 1972. They continued to pay the property taxes and repaired things as they wore out. I think that Mom was seriously thinking about moving back to Grantsville one day. However, this never happened. One of the saddest days of my life (although I did not fully realize the true gravity of the situation until much later in life) was the day in 1982 when an estate auction was held. Nearly all of Grandma's wonderful antiques were whisked away by the highest bidder and many of the old memories went along with them.

Although Andy and I have some of the original furnishings, most were sold. I wish I could have kept everything, or better yet, that the house could have been converted into a Bed and Breakfast with all of the furniture and belongings kept in tact. Then, at least, I could have stayed there from time to time as a guest and relive my childhood memories surrounded by familiar objects. However, the settlement of Grandma's estate occurred long before "Bed and Breakfast" inns became popular. And, financially, it was impossible for anyone in the family to continue to keep the house as it was, or to store all of its treasures. Today, the house is privately owned by others and a small tax service is operated within the residence.

CHAPTER 4

A FRUITFUL AND FLOWERY BACKYARD

*G*randma's backyard was a horticulturalist's dream and a child's delight. It was a place that increased my childhood happiness immensely, not only because I had many fun times there, but also because it was a beautiful and fascinating place. Like the house, the backyard seemed enormous to me at that time. My younger brothers, Danny Davis (my first cousin), and I spent many happy hours there. If we weren't riding our bikes to Pennsylvania or running around the streets of Grantsville, we were playing in the backyard. It was fortunate for our parents that we found so much excitement so close to home.

The most incredible thing about the backyard was that it contained nearly every fruit tree imaginable. I am sure that it was unique compared to other backyards that existed in Grantsville. A gargantuan white cherry tree grew there just outside of Grandma's cement stoop. For those of you who are not familiar with the word "stoop," it is a small porch with steps that serve as the entrance to a house. There were always hundreds of chubby white and pink cherries lying on the ground beneath the tree. Many ended up as tasty morsels for the birds. These cherries were so sweet and I suspect that their sugary fluids were also food for the tiny "piss" ants (as Grandma lovingly called them) that scurried about on the cement stoop and driveway all summer long.

In addition to the white cherry, there was a red cherry tree. This tree was really within the boundary of my parent's small backyard, but all land ran together for "us kids!" These cherries occasionally ended up in a pie, but they also became easy targets for sharp bird beaks. One lone black cherry tree stood in a far corner of the yard. There was also a Bartlett pear tree which bore large, green, and "pearfectly" wonderful fruit. We loved to climb this tree and hide in its branches.

Grape Arbor and Fruit Trees

A graceful grape arbor about 30 yards long led from just outside of Grandmother's house to the barn. This arbor supported large bunches of succulent purple Concord grapes late into the fall. A big purple plum tree grew a short distance from my parent's small, one-car garage. The plums produced by this tree were exquisite --- sweet and firm.

Two gigantic tart, red apple trees occupied a goodly portion of land in the backyard. The apples would fall from the trees, and I occasionally searched the ground for one to eat that wasn't bruised, rotten, or marred by worm holes or bird pecks. It wasn't easy. There was also a rectangular patch of rhubarb growing along a fence near the pear tree. Grandma used to cook rhubarb and I liked how she prepared it. She cooked the long red and green stalks the Amish way, boiling small chunks in water, cornstarch, and sugar until soft.

The backyard not only was the home for a variety of fruit trees, but it also grew many flowering plants. Two beautiful, light purple lilac trees adorned an area by the back fence. I have always loved the scent of lilacs. There were several large, bushy Yew trees, a row of Lilies of the Valley, and Madonna Lilies. Growing along the fence, which paralleled the back alley, were orange snapdragons that I loved to snap. I guess this habit forming "stress reliever" was akin to people today snapping bubble wrap packaging. My brothers and I spent hours building tiny chairs and things by sticking together round, bristly, brown burrs from a weed that also grew along this fence. From this activity, I should have invented Velcro. If only I had known!

There was a long row of peonies of different brightly colored hues of pink. Huge, dazzling, fragrant flowers perched atop stubby, dark green bushes. This row of flowers was the only demarcation between Grandma's yard and our yard. As beautiful as these flowers were, they always had billions of "piss" ants crawling all over them! To bring a bouquet of them into the house would have created an insect invasion of biblical proportions.

Grandma's Peonies

A beautiful, bright orange trumpet vine twisted and curled around a large faded, gray, wood arbor from which a long, wooden swing was suspended. We spent many hours on this swing snapping freshly picked green beans, and sometimes watching the colorful, fast-moving, hummingbirds which were attracted to the vine.

There were also several different varieties and colors of rosebushes in the backyard. One variety was a rather large and thorny, climbing rosebush --- I know because I crashed into it while I was learning to ride my bicycle. I will discuss this traumatic episode in greater detail later.

Grandma's Backyard Swing

Finally, there were two very important structures in the backyard. They were important because they were fun places for "us kids" to be! The first was the big, green barn (the same vibrant green as the house), which stood at the far end of the yard. It no longer sheltered animals, as it once had, but, still contained tons of old hay. By today's standards, it would have been considered a real fire hazard. The barn also contained old farm equipment --- pitch forks, shovels, wheel barrels, horse yokes and harnesses, and a myriad of rusty, dusty old tools whose original purpose could only be discerned by an expert, but which, nevertheless, would sell for "big bucks" at an antique farm equipment auction today.

Barn and Clubhouse, 1962

My brothers, Cousin Danny, and I spent hours rummaging around in the barn or jumping up and down in the dusty hay. The main purpose for the barn, however, was for use as an oversized garage for a vehicle of some sort --- usually someone's family car.

The second important building in the backyard was the little, green clubhouse. It was once used as a chicken house, but we turned it into our backyard hide-a-way. It was like a "tree" house but it was on the ground. It was located right next to the barn and was the same green color as the barn and the house. This little building only had a few very tiny windows and no electricity, so we played inside only during the daylight hours.

We loved this little fortress and would spend hours in it. Periodically we would perform little plays for which we had the audacity to charge admission! Of course, the proceeds were spent immediately after the play on sodas and potato chips. Sadly, it was usually only Aunt Jane (Danny's Mom) who attended. But we sure had fun dreaming up skits and rehearsing. Our stage curtain was a large, white, bed sheet hung from the ceiling. And reminiscent of an old "Little Rascals" television show, we would occasionally get mad at each other and divide the clubhouse in half with a rope or string of some sort. Greg and Bill would stay on one side and Danny and I would stay on the other side. We were not allowed to touch any part of the forbidden side. The little, green clubhouse was a big part of my childhood in Grantsville. I am saddened that the barn and clubhouse have been torn down. They now exist only in my memory.

CHAPTER 5

DAD

*M*y father, Lawrence Sherwood Faith, was born and raised in Hancock, Washington County, Maryland, another small town located on U.S. Route 40, about 60 miles east of Grantsville. He was born March 14, 1917, into a very large family consisting of fifteen brothers and sisters. His father was Harry Erastus Faith; his mother was Bertha Elizabeth Faith, nee Barnhart.

Harry Erastus worked for over 40 years in a sand quarry where, among other things, he set off explosives. My Dad referred to his father as a "quarry engineer." Bertha was a homemaker. Although Harry was gainfully employed, they were quite poor. They lived and raised this large family on a small farmstead adjacent to the C & O Canal. Grandpa Faith commuted to work everyday by rowing a boat across the Potomac River to the West Virginia sand mines.

In contrast to the Davis and Lomison families, there are few photographs of Dad's parents or siblings. I deeply regret that of all of these aunts and uncles, I met only four --- Emma (on her death bed), Melvin, Stanley, and Reda. Emma passed away many years ago. Melvin was killed in a horrific car accident, and Stanley died of pancreatic cancer, as did my Dad. I recently had the good fortune to spend an afternoon with Reda, the youngest of Dad's siblings, who still lives in Hancock. I wanted to meet Reda in order to obtain more information about the Faith family. Sadly, she suffers from dementia and was unable to provide any information about her family.

I know less about the Faith family than the Davis family. The only way for me to learn more about my father's side of the family is to conduct a genealogical study. This project, started in late 2009, is currently underway in collaboration with my brother, Andy and the assistance of my husband, David. For more than 30 years, David has been involved in an in-depth genealogical study of his own family, the Traugers. Overtime, he has discovered that he has hundreds of family members across the country and indeed, all over the world and more are identified every year.

Because of Dad's large family, I am sure that I must have many relatives sprinkled across the United States. Whenever David and I travel to a new place, he will look in a local telephone book for both the Trauger and the Faith surnames. When we find the name of Faith, I wonder if they might be long lost cousins. Dad used to tease me by claiming that we were related to Percy Faith, the late, well-known orchestra conductor. I am not so sure he was teasing now.

Considering my father's impoverished family roots and the fact that he grew up during the Great Depression, it is quite remarkable that he managed not only to attend college, but also to graduate! He was a student at Frostburg State Teacher's College for two years. Dad then transferred to the University of Maryland in College Park, where he received his Bachelor's Degree in Agriculture in 1939. To earn extra money, Dad waited tables in the university's dining hall. There, he met my mother in 1937. Years later, he attended Columbia University, where he received an advanced professional teaching certificate in 1963.

Following Dad's graduation from the University of Maryland, my parents married on July 31, 1939. After their marriage, they moved to the town of Ridgely on the Eastern Shore of Maryland. In the fall of 1939, Dad began a long career teaching high school agriculture.

Lawrence Sherwood Faith, Circa 1939

Mom and Dad first lived in Ridgely from 1939 to 1941. They then relocated to Taneytown, Maryland, where Dad taught from the fall of 1941 to 1942. According to Uncle Bob, Mom was a waitress at a local restaurant. They pulled up stakes again in 1942, and moved to a farm, located just outside of Grantsville, which my Grandfather had purchased. Andy was born on that farm in 1943.

During 1942-1943, Dad taught at Grantsville High School. Before I started school, the High School building in Grantsville where Dad taught was converted to the Grantsville Elementary School, which I attended for six years.

Early in 1944, when Andy was just a few months old, Mom and Dad moved again to Davidsville, Pennsylvania. They lived in an apartment there until they moved onto a 13-acre farm that Grandfather purchased just outside of Davidsville. It is amazing that back then, a 13-acre farm in this beautiful part of the country only cost $6,000!

Dad taught vocational agriculture at Conemaugh Township High School near Davidsville from 1944 until 1945, when Dad was drafted into the United States Army. Dad entered this new chapter of his life reluctantly. In fact, Mom revealed to me later, he went in "kicking and screaming."

Dad was sworn into the United States Army on April 19, 1945. An aptitude test was given to all new inductees, and Dad's test scores revealed a "talent" for the repair of instruments. As a result, he spent twelve weeks at Aberdeen Proving Ground in Maryland, where he received training as an instrument repairman. Dad used this skill in civilian life, teaching both agriculture and industrial arts at Northern High School.

Dad was fairly handy fixing things around the house. Mom told me that he even built a chest of drawers and "put the handles on and everything." But Dad did have the occasional blunder. I remember the day he decided to repair an old, round white, electric clock that hung in our kitchen in Catonsville, Maryland. He kept cutting the electrical cord making it shorter and shorter! I am not sure why he was doing this surgery to the clock, but it was never the same after it had been "repaired."

Upon completion of his 12-week training course at Aberdeen, Dad was sent to Fort Jackson in South Carolina. Unlike my Grandfather, Dad's short stint in the military was rather unremarkable. He only obtained the rank of Private First Class and, although he had been trained in a specific skill, he was given the official title of "General Clerk." As a General Clerk, Dad was given the lofty duties of peeling potatoes, posting venereal disease posters in the latrines, and being the driver for the Commanding Officer. Dad was never given any military medals; however, he did leave the service with a stainless steal, U.S. Army fork --- perhaps a memento from his kitchen patrol duties! He was honorably discharged on April 15, 1946.

While Dad was away in the Army, Mom returned to Grantsville with Andy to live with her parents. Upon Dad's return from the Army, my parents moved into a three-level apartment located directly adjacent to Grandma's house, in a building owned by my Grandfather. This building was the site of Davis family commercial enterprises on the main level. Uncle Bob's family lived in a rather large upstairs apartment in the same building.

In 1947, Dad and Uncle Bob with the financial help of Grandfather Davis began operating a small grocery store called the Grantsville Clover Farm Market. This grocery business lasted for about one year, followed in 1948 by the Davis Hardware Store. Uncle Bob operated the hardware store from 1948 until he sold it in 1972.

Davis Hardware Store

Although Dad and Uncle Bob were business "partners" for a while, somewhere along the way, there may have been a falling out between them. Dad left the hardware store never to return. Following this "parting of the ways," Dad began to teach again. He commuted to Somerset, Pennsylvania, where he taught agriculture to veterans. When this job ended, he obtained a position at Northern High School, where he taught both agriculture and industrial arts.

Northern High School was established in the early 1950's near Accident, Maryland. This school, located about 15 miles southwest of Grantsville, was a consolidated school for students in northern Garrett County. Dad taught there into the early 1960's. He was also instrumental in guiding the Future Farmer's of America (FFA) Program at the high school.

Incidentally, Northern High School is where I began my "illustrious" junior high school career.

For whatever reasons, my impression was that Dad probably drank too much. He may have been an alcoholic. His beverage of choice was beer. When metal cans became popular, I hated the sound of pull-tabs because they signaled another uncertain evening in the Faith household. Dad was never abusive, but he never hugged me or told me that he loved me either. I don't remember ever having a meaningful conversation with him, except later in his life when he had stopped drinking and was very sick with pancreatic cancer and congestive heart failure. I don't recall Dad ever talking about his family or himself in our conversations. He was just a person who lived in the house, I knew that he was my Dad, but there was never a strong father-daughter bond between us.

Although Dad never hurt or abused me, I was sometimes afraid of him. I never knew what he was going to do when he began to drink. I used to hide from him, although I now know I didn't really need to do this. Fortunately, while we lived in Grantsville, Greg, Bill and I spent most of our time running around outside. Mom bore the brunt of Dad's affliction throughout their long marriage. Sadly, Mom was the enabler to Dad's disease. As we children grew older, we too became enablers. I sometimes wonder whether, if we had all ganged up on him and confronted him about his drinking problem it would have made a difference. Perhaps he would have sought help, but I seriously doubt that he would have. The only reason that he stopped drinking was "doctors orders" and his impending death. I recall one time in our house in Catonsville, Andy and I searched the house and collected all of the "booze" we could find and poured it down the kitchen drain. That was as bold as we ever got.

It wasn't until after our time in Grantsville, when I was older, that Dad's beer consumption was a much greater strain on me psychologically. For instance, I never invited friends over because I never knew what sort of shape Dad would be in. Dad was sometimes a disappointment, embarrassment and worry to me in my teenage years. Sometimes he would drink too much, and then call people on the phone. It was obvious to anyone he reached that he was drunk. I hated it when he did this. I also remember a time when a former boyfriend wanted to talk to Dad "man-to-man." My friend was afraid and unable to talk to his own father who was somewhat of a military-type tyrant. Open, frank, discussions were not his father's forte, so my friend attempted to talk to my Dad. But Dad had one too many and the conversation ended up being somewhat incoherent and very one-sided. My young friend certainly did not get the help that he seemed to desperately need at the time.

My Dad was a short, thin, wiry man with very dark brown eyes. He had wavy gray hair, although his hair was dark brown in his younger years. I inherited his hair and his dark eyes. As a young man, he probably weighted 140 pounds soaking wet, and weighed even less in later years, especially in the last years of his life when he was very sick. He was quite handsome, especially when he was younger.

Dad's looks were slightly altered one cold winter morning when he was injured in an automobile accident. He was driving home from visiting a student. He rounded the curve of an unplowed snowy rural road just outside of Grantsville, and collided with an oncoming car. Because neither car could move over (only one lane was plowed), they ran head-on into each other. Dad hit the steering wheel and his mouth was permanently rearranged. He had several subsequent operations, but never looked quite the same, and I am not sure that his dentures ever fit properly after the accident. I still remember being awakened by loud, scary, pounding on our front door the morning of the accident. Although Mom shielded us from the facts and trauma of this event, I knew something "bad" had happened. Mom did not let us go to see him in the hospital. Perhaps she felt we were too young and would have been frightened to see our Dad in such a state.

Dad was among the middle children of a very large family, which must have been extraordinarily difficult. I believe that he felt "lost" his entire life. I have no idea what sort of relationship he had with his own father, but according to Uncle Bob, Grandfather Erastus occasionally visited Dad in Grantsville. I think that Dad struggled all of his life with his identity, and as a result, he was somewhat insecure. My Mom told me that once during a job interview, Dad refused to look the interviewer in the eyes. I believe that part of his insecurity may have stemmed from the fact that he was not a very big man. Dad did not get along with everyone, but he did have a close circle of friends.

I do not want to give the wrong impression about Dad. He had many wonderful attributes. Mom was such a special and intelligent person, that if Dad had not possessed so many special qualities, I doubt she would have ever married him. In spite of his alcoholism, he rose above a deprived childhood and achieved his potential. He graduated from college and completed post-graduate work to become an admired and successful teacher. He was accomplished in several avocations, i.e., horticulture, gardening, wine making, raising and caring for chickens, and cooking.

Dad, Budding Horticulturalist

Dad was very intelligent and could be "standup comedian" funny. He had a quick wit, could tell a great joke, and was also good at doing impersonations. Mom told me that he could give great speeches and that everyone around him would become mesmerized by what he was saying. In his younger years, he was no doubt quite charismatic.

Dad was an avid gardener. He grew a variety of vegetables that supplied fresh and nutritious produce to feed our family. His tomato plants were the envy of the neighborhood. He was also a very talented horticulturalist. He knew exactly what to do to revive a dying plant, how to grow seedlings, or what those funny looking black bugs were on a plant and how to get rid of them. He knew the answer for most questions involving growing green things.

He was also a talented teacher and earned the respect of his students. To his credit, he not only taught high school students for many years, but he also taught night school to veterans for a period of time. In later years, I met former students who talked about Dad as an excellent and caring teacher. A sister of one of his students told me that Dad's influence was the reason that her brother went on to receive his Ph.D. in Agriculture.

In addition to teaching agriculture and industrial arts classes at Northern High School, Dad also taught courses in support of the FFA. He was proud of his soil-judging teams, who always did well in state competitions. In conjunction with his FFA duties, Dad was a judge at the Garrett County Fair, where he selected prize-winning poultry.

Dad was somewhat of an entrepreneur in that he started his own egg-production enterprise. A huge white, egg-shaped sign with big black letters that read "FRESH EGGS" hung from a tall silver pole outside of our house in Grantsville. Many people stopped by our house to purchase one or two dozen of these fragile-shelled beauties. Father's flair for entrepreneurship began as a young boy when he hatched a scheme to make money by trapping muskrats. He described his anticipation of making a fortune as he sent the first dried hide to a furrier and his great disappointment when he got the pelt back with a note saying: "One mouse hide --- worthless."

In addition to teaching agriculture, Dad also taught general science at Catonsville Junior High School and later horticulture at Lansdowne High School in Baltimore County. His obituary reads: "Although he was a senior teacher, he always took the general and vocational classes, feeling a special compassion for children who were difficult to motivate." As told to me by a cousin, Dad once made some "rowdy" students remove some inappropriate words from a chalkboard. He gave the students spray bottles filled with a clear liquid for this purpose. The students said, "This stuff is great, Mr. Faith --- it really works! What is it?" Dad replied, "H2O!"

Last, but certainly not least, Dad was a good cook. He often helped Mom in the kitchen with the preparation of family meals. One of his specialties was boiled shrimp. He used to boil shrimp in beer late at night. I would smell the steaming concoction and tip-toe downstairs. We would peel and eat shrimp on the kitchen table that he had earlier prepared by laying down sheets of newspapers for our fine feast. When we were finished eating, only large piles of empty, opaque pink shrimp shells with little white legs remained. I love to eat boiled shrimp to this day. Nowadays, I am more concerned with how my fingers smell afterwards. Peeling boiled shrimp is not as "appealing" to me as it once was when I was sharing "shrimp" time with Dad.

Dad had many wonderful attributes. Unfortunately, I think the rest of the world, especially his students, saw most of them; not his family. Although I saw occasional glimpses of compassion, it was not very often. Once he made me hot tea when I was sick without my even asking him to do it. Mostly, we merely tolerated each other depending on the situation

Dad's Shrimp Recipe

1 pound shrimp in the shell

1 cup white vinegar

1 cup water or beer

1 teaspoon salt

"Hell's of pepper"

A few shakes whole celery seed

Bring mixture to a boil and reduce to a simmer

Add shrimp and cook 30 minutes

Sauce: Mixture of ketchup and horseradish to taste

Chef Larry

It is unfortunate that a man with so much intelligence and talent let alcohol have such a destructive effect on him. Binge drinking over the years probably destroyed some brain cells and may also have damaged his heart. It may have been a contributing factor to his pancreatic cancer. To his credit, Dad quit drinking and stopped smoking on his own later in life. But, unfortunately, the damage had already been done.

I guess that I have come to terms with Dad's beer drinking, but it has been a real struggle for me over the years. I still feel angry with him sometimes. I find myself blaming him when I am unpleasant to someone, or if I don't hug my husband enough, or if I am reluctant to let someone get to know me. I am convinced that if he had been a warm, caring father I would be a better human being. Dad loved us all, I am certain of that, but he had difficulty showing this love. He was not very demonstrative, and I think that, in my case, "the acorn did not fall too far from the oak tree."

Dad had a long struggle with pancreatic cancer. He was fortunate to be able to spend his final months at home where Mom took care of him. On January 27, 1991, Dad passed away. He died in his easy chair in the living room at Catonsville, Maryland. He was cremated and buried in the Grantsville Cemetery in the Davis Family plot.

Upon reflection, I realize now that in spite of everything, he was my Dad. He was always a part of my life, for better or for worse. I know that he loved me, and because of this, I loved him. I am equally certain that the reason I did not cry much when he died was because although I loved him, he was emotionally unattainable to me. Consequently, I really never knew who he was as a person.

CHAPTER 6

MOM

*M*y mother was Florence Vivian Faith, nee Davis. She was born on October 24, 1920 in Henry, West Virginia, a small coal-mining town that no longer exists. Unlike Dad, Mom was born into a small family that was certainly comfortable financially. My Grandfather's medical practice enabled the family to thrive and afforded them the opportunity to have many of the nice things that life had to offer early in the Twentieth Century, including a beautiful home in Grantsville.

Davis House in Henry, West Virginia
Mom was born here; Dr. Davis' Office in rear

My Grandparents moved to Grantsville from West Virginia when Mom was about one year old. Grandfather purchased the family home on Main Street from another medical doctor who had lived there. Members of the Davis family remained there until either a marriage or death intervened.

Mom absolutely adored her Father; she thought he was both a wonderful and honorable man. She also had much love and admiration for her Mother. It is my belief, however, that Mom felt a much stronger bond with her Father than she did with her Mother.

Adoration: Mom with her Dad, Circa 1924

Mom had many delightful memories of her life growing up in Grantsville. She occasionally accompanied her Dad when he visited his patients in their homes. Mom would also help her Dad with gardening and yard chores. She had fond memories of him reading the funny papers to her while she sat curled up in his lap.

When Mom was about eight years old, her Dad bought her a little, red pony. Although my Grandfather could mount this tiny animal and ride him, albeit with his feet dragging on the ground, his daughter was less fortunate. The pony managed to buck her off on more than one occasion. For this reason, she became afraid of the animal and never learned to successfully ride him.

I think that both Mom and my Uncle Bob had happy childhoods. But, they were also mischievous and got into trouble just like all kids do. Mom told the story of how she once hid behind a big chair and cut off all of her hair. Grandma got very angry with her for doing such a stunt. Despite her anger, she saved a lock of Mom's hair as a memento of this childish prank. Mom also told the story of how Bob decided he wanted to taste a pie that was cooling on top of a glass-fronted, corner cupboard on the back porch. He started to climb the tall obstacle that was keeping him from his pie, when the whole thing fell down on top of him --- pie and all!

Mom began her education at the age of five. She started first grade early because her birthday fell in October. Knowing Mom, however, she was no doubt intelligent enough to begin the first grade at that tender age. She attended elementary through high school in Grantsville. She graduated from Grantsville High School in 1937.

Mom then decided that she wanted to attend the University of Maryland at College Park, Maryland. She was enrolled there from 1937 until she quit in 1938, temporarily ending her college career. The explanation she offered was that the University of Maryland was "the most artificial place she had ever experienced" and that she just got fed up with the whole thing. But my perception is that Mom was not ready for college. Besides, she met Dad. Young love has a way of obscuring one's vision, making a situation in which you really don't want to be, seem even more untenable. As Mom perceived her situation, there was absolutely no reason for her to be in college at that time.

Mom was very pretty. She was short, and claimed that she used to be five feet four inches tall, but that she shrank to about five feet two inches. I have doubts about her original height. She had dark brown hair, beautiful blue eyes, and a wonderful figure. Mom always had gorgeous Betty Grable-like legs.

Time and age have a way of rearranging and greatly changing our once young appearance. Besides time and age, Mom not only dealt with many personal tragedies, but also suffered many physical traumas to her body. She endured a complete hysterectomy, breast cancer and resulting double mastectomies, high blood pressure, adult-onset diabetes, cataracts and glaucoma. Mom struggled with very poor circulation, especially in her legs. She underwent two operations on her right leg to increase the circulation in that part of her body, specifically to her right foot. Eventually, she battled congestive heart failure which was the primary reason that full recovery and normal use of her right leg was slow.

I am certain that Mom's life long addiction to tobacco was either an exacerbating factor or the direct cause of some, if not all, of her health problems. I am a former smoker. I quit "cold turkey" in 1986. Although it took me several tries, the final attempt to "kick the habit" was relatively easy and painless. I know it is wrong to assume that just because I quit smoking, anyone can, especially in this case. Mom was deeply addicted to cigarettes, both psychologically and physically. As her daughter, I will always be upset about Mom's smoking habit, but, unfortunately, the damage had been done. I am exceedingly grateful that she did not develop lung cancer or emphysema on top of all her other medical issues.

As mentioned earlier, Mom married Dad on July 31, 1939. They moved around to different areas in Maryland and Pennsylvania, while Dad taught school, but they eventually settled in Grantsville in 1943, where they initially lived on a farm that had been purchased by Grandfather Davis. This farm is still in existence just outside of town and is now owned by an Amish family. Mom had the fun farm duty of washing the milk separators every day. She hated this chore. They lived on the farm for about one year during which time Andy was born. They had milk cows, beef cattle, geese, and chickens. A windmill supplied power to the farm.

Mom and Dad had four children: Andrew Davis Faith, born October 23, 1943, Alice Lorraine Faith, born August 10, 1949, Gregory Oakes Faith and William Cass Faith, born April 1, 1951. Greg and Bill were fraternal twins. Grandfather delivered three of Mom's children. He delivered Andy on the farm outside of Grantsville. He also brought Greg and Bill into the world at our home in Grantsville. Mom explained to me that because she was expecting twins, Grandfather did not "trust" anyone else to deliver them! I was the only baby born in a hospital --- leave it to me to be different!

**Mom and her first born, Andrew
Circa 1945**

Mom and Dad eventually moved into a three-story apartment house that was attached to the Davis Hardware Store and adjoining warehouse. We lived there until leaving Grantsville in 1963. Andy lived next door in Grandma's house because there really wasn't room for him in the apartment. Above the hardware store was another apartment where Mom's brother, my Uncle Bob lived with his wife Jane, and their two children, Bobbi Jane and Danny. I sometimes wonder if the Faith and Davis families flipped a coin to see which family would live in which apartment.

I think Mom was pretty overwhelmed for quite a long time with her maternal and domestic responsibilities. As if four small children weren't enough, she had to struggle with a variety of personal issues and life events.

Alice   **Greg**   **Bill**
Grade School Photos

Mom had to deal with Dad's occasional bouts of drinking. She also had to tolerate her Mother, who could be irritable and obstinate at times. In addition, Mom served as mediator for all of the members of the three separate households. I believe that there were probably some challenging family dynamics happening over the years in Grantsville. Living in close proximity, as we did, sometimes produces difficulties even among the best of families. I think that Mom had to walk a fine line in order to make everyone happy and also keep her own sanity. Thinking back, I do not remember Grandma ever stepping foot inside of our apartment! I am not sure of this, but I don't believe she was ever very happy with Mom's partner in marriage. I don't remember Dad being in Grandma's house very often either.

It was during this tumultuous time in Mom's life that she had a very unique and unusual experience. I believe it was a life-altering event for her. This unusual experience was a true moment of intellectual enlightenment or illumination, which I believe for that instant in time, for whatever reason, placed Mom on another plane of existence.

This event happened around 1955. As she told the story, Mom had been washing clothes in the basement and "came tearing up the basement steps" and was standing next to a table by the kitchen sink. All of a sudden a bright light appeared from above and bathed her in light. Tiny grains of white sand began to appear and fell down upon her as though she were standing inside of an hourglass. Mom said that the grains of sand appeared so real that she was compelled to reach out to touch them but she felt nothing. At this moment, Mom said that she felt omniscient --- that she knew everything and that all life flowed in a circle. This profound enlightenment was about an ancient concept: the circle of life. This experience was a wonderful, extraordinary event for Mom. She may have been stressed to the "max" and hallucinating with four small children and many other problems. Whatever the explanation, the event did happen to her.

This was a defining moment for Mom. It is my understanding that what she experienced has happened to many other extraordinary individuals over the ages. Believe it or not, I know that this occurrence remained a permanent part of Mom's psyche for the rest of her life.

Mom always wondered whether or not she should have done something special with this remarkable event. In a way, I think she did. Mom managed to live through many personal tragedies over the years, experiences that I believe would have destroyed many people. She also managed to maintain an inner core of strength from which others have drawn fortitude. Mom was an exceptional woman. If it hadn't been for her, I do not believe that I would be as strong and as "normal" as I am today.

I don't know if this event in Mom's early life caused her to be this way or if it merely strengthened her resolve, but throughout her life, she was very intuitive and in touch with herself --- much more than I am. I seem to find things out after the fact, never realizing what is really going on. I perceived Mom as being extraordinarily spiritual, and I do not mean in the religious sense of the word. Our family was not religious and we did not belong to any of the local churches. Out of curiosity, I attended Sunday School a few times at the Lutheran Church, but Mom and Dad were not church goers.

She had always been "out there" about things such as unidentified flying saucers (UFOs), ghosts, and extrasensory perception (ESP), just to name a few. She greatly admired "psychic" Edgar Cayce and talked about him often. These were some of the wonderful things about Mom: her mind was open to all of the possibilities of life. She "knew" things about people that later turned out to be true --- such things as illnesses or even well hidden sexual orientations. She was very aware of true feelings and saw behind the "masks" that some people use in order to disguise their true identities.

It was while Mom was staying home taking care of her children and being a housewife that she came up with what she thought was a brilliant idea. She could not stand it when bars of soap eventually disintegrated into small, slippery hard-to-hold, chunks and chips. She would end up throwing away many slimy slivers of soap, which she thought was a waste. She came up with the concept of placing a small piece of soap-shaped plastic inside of each bar of soap. This would enable the user to not only use the soap down to the last bubble but in addition, the piece of plastic could be reused in some way. This idea was similar to the notion of finding a plastic toy in a Cracker Jack box.

Mom decided to take her exciting idea to Mr. Joe Fahey who worked at the First State Bank on Main Street. When she finished telling Joe about her new invention, he just looked at her and said, "Florence, you need to go back to school and get your teaching degree at Frostburg State College." Mom took this statement as a challenge and returned to college to finish her degree. She graduated from Frostburg State Teachers College in 1961 with a Bachelor's Degree in education and her teaching certification. Mr. Fahey's belief that Mom was an intelligent young woman with potential turned out to be well founded.

Mom's College Graduation Picture

It is extraordinarily ironic that some 50 years after Mom's exchange with Mr. Fahey in the bank, I turned this same old brick building into the Grantsville Community Museum. This corner building has had several incarnations. After its long existence as the First State Bank of Grantsville, it was transformed into a branch of the Ruth Enlow Library. As a library, the walls were lined with pink bookcases and the floors were covered with old, glued down carpeting. It took a tremendous amount of renovation and hard work to create a museum for the community but the task was finally accomplished. Today, Grantsville has a beautiful little museum of which it can be very proud. I am no longer the curator, but I have given back something special to the town which gave me so much as a young child.

After graduation, Mom taught for one year at nearby Long Stretch Elementary School, then transferred to an elementary school in Accident, Maryland, where she taught first and second grade. She really enjoyed this teaching assignment, but once again found herself somewhat overwhelmed. Mom was very conscientious in everything that she did. I am sure that she wanted to be "all that she could be" in the teaching profession. She worked diligently to prepare for daily teaching lessons. In order to do this, Mom was taking work home; she was grading papers, preparing lesson plans, and probably a myriad of other tasks that are necessary when teaching children in a classroom setting. But, she was also still taking care of her home and raising her children.

In addition to all of this, Dad was in "hot water" with the Superintendent of Schools for Garrett County. The Superintendent was evidently one of the people with whom he could not get along. At any rate, Dad ended up getting fired from his job, and Mom, who was no doubt doing an excellent job at her teaching position, was fired too! I think the term for this is "guilt by association," or in this situation, "fired by association." This must have been a very difficult, painful, and embarrassing situation for Mom. Nevertheless, she had to find the strength to carry on. She did. Mom went to work at the Grantsville Brick Plant, where she worked as a bookkeeper for about a year.

Shortly after the school-firing fiasco in 1963, the family moved to the Baltimore area (although we also considered Eugene, Oregon). I think the move was mostly to "escape" Garrett County and begin a new life.

When we moved down to Baltimore County, Mom resumed her teaching career. She taught briefly at Johnny Cake Elementary School and then at Halethorpe Elementary School. She eventually quit teaching and began working as a claims examiner with the Social Security Administration in Woodlawn, Maryland.

Mom died during the writing of this book. The last time I saw her alive was on October 9, 2000. When I left, my final words to her were, "I love you, Mom." Her only response was a slight nodding of her head. But I am sure she understood what I said. As a result, I stopped working on the book for many years. I knew that it would be too painful for me to continue. When I began to write again, it was important for me to go back and revise the wording to reflect Mom's passing.

CHAPTER 7

MY THREE BROTHERS

I have one older brother, Andy, who is still living, and two younger brothers, Greg and Bill, who both passed away in 1988. I wish that Andy and I had been closer as brother and sister when we were growing up, but our entire lives seem to have been on separate tracks. I attribute our emotional distance to not only our separate upbringing, but also to our age difference. He is six years older than me, and he was not a big part of my early life. I was only 12 when he went off to college at the University of Maryland in College Park, Maryland. There he received his Bachelor's Degree in Journalism in 1965 and then on to his own life. He married Bonnie Sansom on June 4, 1966, when I was 16 years old.

Big Brother Andy, November 1958

Despite our separate lives, Andy has been there for me in the past and I know that he will be there for me always, no matter what. One Friday night, I had gotten all dolled up to go to a teen dance at the American Legion building which was located toward the east end of town. I absolutely loved to go there, because I was able to dance for hours. Every Friday evening, the Legion Hall was opened up to the teenagers of Grantsville.

You must understand that the fashion in the early 1960's was big, teased up hair. Well, my hair was teased all right, to about a foot tall. I don't think that I even combed it down very much --- it must have looked like a rat's nest! In addition, I was wearing a very short skirt and had applied pale lipstick: almost white (another hot look in the 1960's).

Anyway, I thought I was the most gorgeous thing on the planet and was standing in the kitchen getting ready to walk out the front door when Mom stopped me. I know she was concerned about my appearance, and thinking back, I'm sure I must have looked a fright. Andy happened to be there, and he argued in my defense. He told Mom that I looked fine and to let me go. She did.

Andy was a successful managing editor for the Baltimore Sun newspaper for many years. He and Bonnie have remained married for over 40 years! That is certainly more than most of us can say. Andy is a very kind, caring, warm, and an exceptionally intelligent individual. He lived in Catonsville, just a few miles away from Mom. He was absolutely wonderful to her and was always there whenever she needed him. He has also raised two sons, Greg and Tim, who have successfully developed their own unique careers. As of this writing, there are no grandchildren for Andy and Bonnie.

Andy and Bonnie on Wedding Day

After Mom passed away, Andy and Bonnie moved to Bel Air, Maryland just north of Baltimore. He continued to work for the Sun for a few more years before he retired in August 2008. In recent years, I am happy to say that Andy and I have become closer and share a love of family genealogy. Andy has been working diligently on the Davis Family Tree and we have discovered many exciting new pieces of information, including the location of several important gravesites. Andy is my beloved big brother.

Greg and Bill are very special to me as well. From my earliest memory, they were my constant companions. We did everything together. We rode our bikes together, played in the clubhouse, climbed trees, got wet on our bright yellow Slip-and-Slide, played "Three Bears Out Tonight," had painful apple fights, collected caterpillars in our little red wagon (and then drowned them in boiling hot water), washed the sidewalk in front of our house on our hands and knees, went trick-or-treating, had snowball fights, built tanks out of discarded refrigerator cardboard boxes, played with our train set, went sledding, built snowmen, made snow tunnels, among the thousands of other things that we did over the years. They were always by my side. Now I must reveal my spiritual side --- I hope they still are.

Inevitably, we went our separate ways, I am not sure exactly when or why that happened. Because I was a couple of years ahead of Greg and Bill in school, junior high school was a likely starting point. The three of us did our "own thing" in high school. When I married for the first time at the age of 19 and moved away from home, the relationship with my two younger brothers became more distant. I was gone, never to return, except for occasional visits, to the house in Catonsville. Our childhood closeness vanished forever.

Bill   **Greg**
Junior High School Pictures

Bill attended the University of Maryland - Baltimore County (UMBC) for his undergraduate degree. He received his Bachelor of Science degree in chemistry in 1973. He earned his Master's degree in pharmacology at the University of Maryland at Baltimore in 1976, and a Doctoral degree in medicinal chemistry at the University of Connecticut in 1982. He completed postdoctoral research at Brandeis University in 1984. Bill began his career as a research scientist at the National Cancer Institute's Cancer Research Facility at Fort Detrick in Frederick, Maryland. He continued his work as a research scientist of medicinal chemistry at Rorer Group Incorporated, a pharmaceutical firm in Fort Washington, Pennsylvania. He developed a number of compounds, including a heart medication that was in the process of being patented for use in the United States and Europe at the time of his death.

Greg also attended the University of Maryland - Baltimore County (UMBC) and received his Bachelor of Science degree in chemistry in 1973. He graduated Cum Laude. He then attended Johns Hopkins University for a short while before being accepted into the University of Maryland at Baltimore School of Medicine. Greg graduated on June 2, 1978, at which time he received his medical degree. He completed his medical internship at Union Memorial Hospital in Baltimore, Maryland.

Greg became a successful doctor in internal medicine. Although he practiced briefly at a medical clinic on the Eastern Shore of Maryland, his last position was with an emergency clinic located in Texas. The staff there absolutely adored him as evidenced by the following statement that was printed in a newsletter at the time of his tragic death: "Being associated with Dr. Faith was indeed a pleasure for me. He was a man who dedicated himself to the practice of medicine and to helping other people with their problems. I can honestly say that in the five years that I was associated with Dr. Faith, I never once heard him utter a disparaging word against another person. His kindness and his gentle manner were his source of strength. He will be missed."

Bill and Greg both passed away in 1988; they were only 37 years old. Bill died after a long fight with brain cancer in April of 1988. In 1987 Bill was diagnosed with a Grade 3 Astrocytoma, non-dominant, frontal lobe "terminal" brain cancer. After his brain surgery, Mom took care of him in her home for about a year until he died. There was no history of brain cancer in our family, so I often wondered if he had occupational exposure to some chemical or biological agent. We have subsequently learned about a "cancer cluster" around Fort Detrick that may be a link to his illness. This cluster is currently being investigated by the U.S. Environmental Protection Agency (EPA).

Greg died after a long battle with Acquired Immune Deficiency Syndrome (AIDS) in December of 1988. Although they were fraternal twins, they had different sexual orientations. Greg tried valiantly to hide his "secret" from the family his entire life. He even dated girls throughout high school. However, the truth finally surfaced after he became gravely ill. When Mom and I had to don facemasks and other protective clothing in order to see him in his hospital room --- we knew. At least, that's when I knew for sure. Mom, I am convinced, knew long before Greg became terminally ill. But neither Mom nor I had to guess about Greg's lifestyle after this visit. While Greg was lying in his hospital bed, he put one of his hands on top of my hand and his other hand on top of Mom's hand and told us point blank, "Mom,

Alice, I'm gay." During this difficult time, I asked Greg when he knew that he was gay and he told me that he realized it when he was just a little boy. In that split second, I understood that some humans are just born this way.

Greg and Bill were the most kind, generous, intelligent, loving brothers that a sister could have. I loved them dearly, and I know that their deaths were a terrible loss to our world. They both had tremendous potential to make great strides in the fields of chemistry and medicine. I would do anything to be able to talk to them again.

One final loving memory about my brothers … Greg and Bill had a difficult time pronouncing my name when they were small, it came out as either "Icy" or as "Wuzzy." To this day, Andy still occasionally calls me Wuzzy or Wuz. Even Mom had been known to address a letter to me as "Dearest Wuz." Greg and Bill are gone from this earth but not from our hearts.

CHAPTER 8

MY HUMBLE HOME

One could not possibly compare my Grandmother's large beautiful house to the home in which I grew up, because there was absolutely no resemblance between the two.

We lived in a rather simple, unadorned apartment. But it was comfortable enough and it certainly provided adequate shelter for the family for many years. While I lived in that home, there was an open front porch with a small set of stairs. Today, no front porch exists on this building. The inside of the apartment was also completely renovated many years ago, shortly after we moved out in 1963.

Faith Family Home, left rear; Uncle Bob's Home, above right

My home had three floors. The first level was a cellar. Unlike Grandma's cellar that frightened me, I just didn't like our cellar. It was just an old cellar and I was down there as little as possible. It had fifteen or so wooden steps that led down to this rather small area of the house. The cellar had a cement floor and the walls were constructed of rather large, rough, stone blocks. Our clothes washer and dryer were down there. Lots of things were also stored on plain, wooden shelves that we did not have space for in the house. In addition, Dad had his blue and red egg-grading machine and egg-washing machine down there.

**Bill, Alice, and Greg with Little Red Wagon
and Mom's Fresh Wash**

The one unique thing about our tiny cellar was that there were uneven, stone steps that led to the outside and into our backyard. The door was fashioned much like a bomb or tornado shelter door in that it opened on a slant and was quite heavy. If I remember correctly, it was held open with a large hook and eye sort of arrangement. This is how Mom took out the laundry to be hung up and dried. And she did loads of laundry. I used to watch her walk back and forth with a wet rag firmly holding on to each of the clotheslines in order to get them clean. Long skinny black stripes appeared on the wet rag after each trip across the lawn. Dad occasionally shared in this wash day chore.

The first floor of the house was where the living room, dining area, kitchen, and back porch were located. The front porch entrance led directly into the living room. This area had several large chairs, an end table or two, a couch, a coffee table, two bookcases (one built in and one free standing). We also had our black and white television that stood in one corner of the room. When I was very young, I spent many hours in front of this new invention watching "Captain Kangaroo" and "Howdy Doody," and as I grew older, I loved to watch "American Bandstand." Watching the kids dance on this show is how I first learned the steps to all of the popular dances of the day --- the Pony, the Bristol Stomp, the Mashed Potatoes, and, of course, the Twist. I also learned all of the old standards like the Jitterbug, the Cha Cha, and the Stroll --- I can still hear Fats Domino singing "Walking to New Orleans."

One way that I practiced "fast" dancing, especially the Jitterbug was to tie a long piece of string to a doorknob and that would be my "partner." I would also practice with a girlfriend, Pam Delligetti, who lived directly across from Grandma's house. Pam and her family moved down from Connellsville, Pennsylvania. Her family rented the apartment above the adjacent small five-and-dime variety store. We would dance for hours dreaming up new, fancy routines.

The apartment and store no longer exist where Pam and her family lived. This family seemed to "stand out" in our small town. I think that they were probably the only Italian family living in Grantsville at that time. Pam's father had such black hair and the whole family had olive-colored complexions. Pam used to call women's headscarves "babushkas." I thought it was such a funny sounding word. To this day, when I hear this word, I think of Pam and our time in Grantsville.

Our living room was very basic, certainly nothing fancy. I guess the most wonderful thing about this room, besides our television set, was that every Christmas this is where our enormous Christmas tree would be placed. It always reached the ceiling and each year it seemed to become more beautiful to me. I will tell you more about Christmas at our house in a later chapter.

Upon leaving the living room, one would enter the dining room area. This was where my family ate meals most of the time. We very rarely went out to eat. Occasionally, in the summer, we would have family picnics, but these, too, were far and few between. During a visit to Grantsville many years later, my husband and I asked the couple who established the Savage River Lodge where we were staying, if they could recommend a good place to eat. Their reply was "Grantsville is a culinary wasteland." Can you imagine what it was like forty years earlier! Thank goodness, we had our garden and Dad had his chickens.

Our family always ate meals together, especially at dinnertime --- even Andy joined us. In today's hectic society, this is a highly unusual occurrence in many families. I don't think we had much money, and therefore, meals were usually very simple but always tasty and satisfying, at least they were to me. I recall one meal that we would have occasionally and that was boiled EGGS! We would carefully remove the eggs from their shells and mash them up into hundreds of tiny yellow and white pieces, sprinkle them with salt and pepper, and have a feast. Eggs were certainly one plentiful food item in our house; we had a seemingly endless supply.

Mom in Our Bountiful Garden   Dad tending His Green Beans

We were fortunate in that we had a productive garden that was located just beyond the back alley. We grew all sorts of wonderful fresh vegetables in the rich black soil. Some of these vegetables included green onions and potatoes. But my two favorites were sweet corn and tomatoes. I used to pick the tomatoes right from the vine and eat them on the spot. Needless to say, summer meals were my favorites because we always had fresh green beans, corn-on-the cob, and tomatoes. To this day, I love summer meals and all of the wonderful vegetables ripe from the warm sunny days and gentle summer showers. Amidst all of the vegetables in our garden, were Grandma's beloved tall, glorious, gladiola flowers. To this day, gladiolas are my favorite flower.

Also, the town fire siren was located in the far corner of our garden on top of a tall pole. This alarm went off every Saturday at noon to signal the end of the workweek, as well as every time a fire was reported in the Grantsville area. When this siren blasted for a fire, cars and trucks of all descriptions could be seen racing through the back alley and down Main Street in the direction of the blaze. Not only were these vehicles driven by the volunteer firemen, but always a number of concerned neighbors and curious thrill-seekers.

It was during our summer family dinners that I had my "corn-on-the cob experiences." Andy and I would sometimes have corn-eating contests. We would see who could eat the most ears of corn. We must have sounded and looked like pigs eating at a trough. I would crunch and chomp back and forth on the cob as fast as I could. It was as if I were playing a long yellow harmonica. When we were done eating, our plates held what looked like small pyramids of naked, nubby corncobs. I could eat at least eight, ten, twelve, and sometimes even more ears of corn at one sitting. There is absolutely no way that I could do this today --- I would be pooping out corn kernels for weeks.

During one of these fierce corn competitions, a friend of Andy's arrived for a visit. His name was Johnny Price and I had an enormous crush on him. I thought he was the most handsome boy in the world, even with his crew cut. Of course, I immediately stopped eating my corn, or else I suddenly developed manners. I was so embarrassed to be eating like this in front of Johnny. No contest --- Andy won that round by a landslide! We had many rematches, but I think Andy usually won.

I suppose this is as good a place as any to talk about our town dump, because this is where our many corncobs ended up along with all of our other garbage. For some weird reason the dump scene is permanently etched in my mind. At least once a week or so, we would drive east out of Grantsville. About one half mile from town, we would make a right hand turn and drive down a long road, the name of which escapes me. Dad would stop the car along the side of the road, unload our paper bags of refuse, and with a hearty heave-ho, toss the stuff over the side of a hill. There was garbage everywhere, as far as the eye could see --- tons of it. What an awful eyesore! But this was the way many small towns across America dealt with garbage back in the "good old days."

Although some towns periodically burned the stinky stuff, I do not think that the town of Grantsville burned its garbage. I think that it just rotted away, if it could! Thank goodness for Earth Day. This was the beginning, in 1970, of making such "crimes against nature" an environmental felony. Ugly dumps like the one in Grantsville no longer exist. The fact that we degraded our beautiful environment in this way still upsets me. Unfortunately, there are many acres of land in our nation that are final resting places to old discarded refrigerators, dilapidated couches, rusty cars, and other material possessions no longer desired by the owners. In the quote from Chief Seattle: "The earth does not belong to us, we belong to the earth." When will we learn to take care of our environment? But, I digress.

Our dining room was plainly decorated like the living room. Other than the dining table and chairs, this room was also where our old, white refrigerator was housed. The two things that I vividly remember about the refrigerator were that this is where Mom kept all of the clothes that were to be ironed! She used to sprinkle them with tap water and then roll them into a log shape and stick them in the vegetable crisper drawers. This is also where Mom kept her sizable stash of celery. She seemed to crave this crunchy green vegetable and would eat stalks of it constantly making sure that each stalk was salted to perfection.

A buffet that matched the table and chairs was located in a recessed area of the dining room. The dining room table, chairs, and buffet were made of maple and quite plain in their appearance --- nearly akin to Shaker-style furniture. For a long time, I had this set gathering dust in my basement in Virginia. Unfortunately, in my younger, dumber years, I painted every inch of this furniture black. During our last move and with more than a twinge of remorse, I gave this furniture set to Goodwill.

There was also a tall, built-in china cabinet that reached almost to the ceiling. I guess Mom put things that we didn't use much on the top shelf. Our telephone was located in the dining room. It was one of those old, black rotary telephones. I think that our old telephone may be in the Smithsonian along with Grandma's wringer washing machine. One interesting side note: In those days before area codes, local telephone numbers consisted of only one or two digits.

Mom in Our Kitchen

The kitchen area was right next to the dining room. The whole area was actually just one long, rectangular shaped room but there was a definite demarcation between the two areas. There was a slight sloping of the floor that I don't think was on purpose. The kitchen had all of the usual suspects. It had a sink that was right below a window that faced north. There was an old gas stove, a table with several drawers, an old gray metal filing cabinet, probably full of Dad's teaching materials. I listened to the radio that was placed on top of the filing cabinet.

We also had a tiny room off of the kitchen that served as our pantry. On the door frame of that pantry opening was the area where Dad would periodically measure the height of Greg, Bill, and me. He had us stand tall against the doorframe and then he placed a yard stick level above our head. He would place a small pencil line at that point and write our name and the date next to the mark. I wonder if those pencil marks are still there. I also remember that our kitchen had remarkably ugly linoleum floor covering. It was yellow with all kinds of different colored spots and dots on it. Ugh!

I remember three things about our old gas stove. The first thing was roasting marshmallows over the gas flames of the stove. Greg, Bill, and I would stick big, white marshmallows on long tree twigs that had their ends carved down to a point and get the soft things so close to the blue flames that the whole marshmallow would go up in a fiery, orange and blue blaze. We would quickly blow it out, but not before it had turned almost completely black. We would then eat the charred morsel burning our lips in the process. But these sweet, gooey treats were sure good. Looking back, I am glad we didn't burn the house down.

The second thing was trying to make coffee for Mom and Dad one morning. The boys and I got up before they did and we decided that we would surprise them by making coffee. We used an old drip-style coffee maker --- the type that comes in three sections. We got the coffee grounds properly placed into the middle section and then began pouring water into the top portion. We did not realize that you only had to pour water into the top one time to fill it. Instead, when the water disappeared, we continued to pour water into the top and before long, pale brown water came flooding out of everywhere --- all over the stovetop and onto the floor --- what a mess! I can't recall Mom and Dad's reaction to our first attempt at making coffee.

The third thing about our old gas stove was how we used to make toast. We did not have a conventional toaster, but instead we had an antique looking black thing. The "toaster" looked a little like a man's top hat, only it was slightly tapered at the top and had four distinct flat sides. Each side was perforated with many tiny holes. Also attached along the bottom of each side was a piece of wire that held the bread in place. The "toaster" would be placed over the flames of one burner. You would then place a piece of bread against one side and begin the toasting process. After one side was sufficiently brown you would turn the bread around and place the other side against the toaster. The old thing worked great. Sometimes I wish I had it today; there was nothing that could breakdown!

The last room on this floor was the back porch. Basically, this room was used by us kids as a passageway from the kitchen to the great outdoors. It was a distinctly separate room off of the kitchen as there was a door that opened to it. This room was used primarily to store boxes full of paperwork and books. It also had a square table located in one corner and a narrow bench on which plants rested.

The only neat thing about our back porch was that it had a long, wooden swing suspended from the ceiling that we used quite often, especially during the warm months. This swing was made by Grandmother's Dad, Edmund Lomison, in his home workshop on the farm in central Pennsylvania. Dad's old, wool, olive drab army blanket was also a permanent accessory to the swing.

The Lomison Farm on the Susquehanna River

Mom kept this antique swing on her back porch in Catonsville. However, Uncle Bob replaced the old rusty chains that were the original connections to various ceilings for decades. Bright, shiny, silver chains were affixed, and if the swing still exists, they are no doubt still attached.

Located in one corner of the living room there was a long set of stairs leading to the second floor. The stairs were carpeted with a vertical multi-colored stripe design that made them appear even steeper and longer than they actually were. The carpeting was kept in place with long, metal rods at the base of each step. Mom hung long, green curtains at about the mid-way point in order to keep drafts from flowing up or down the stairs. She would periodically "wipe off" the stair steps by briskly moving a damp rag back and forth over the carpeting. I can still hear the scraping sound that this cleaning chore made on the carpeting. It's funny, that after we moved away Mom never did this tedious task again. I guess she decided to rely on the vacuum cleaner.

Upon reaching the top of the stairs, there was a small landing where you could choose to go left or right after taking one more step up. To the left, was a hallway that led to the only bathroom in the house --- on the right as you walked down the hallway. The bathroom was rather long and rectangular. At one end, were the toilet and a small table. Mom kept some of her things on this table, maybe even some bottles of Evening in Paris perfume. At the other end, there was a sink with a medicine chest above it. In between and against the wall adjacent to the hallway stood a white porcelain, claw-footed bathtub. We had no shower. A north-facing window near the sink, overlooked the slanting, shingled roof of the first floor and the backyard.

When we were very little, Greg, Bill, and I took a bath once a week whether we needed one or not! Of course, we always did. We would be put in the tub at the same time, and Mom and Dad would get down on their knees next to the tub and scrub us down. This was fun for me --- we were being a family. I'm not sure how much fun it was for Mom and Dad though; we must have been quite a handful and slippery, too!

At the end of the hallway was Greg and Bill's bedroom. This room had at least two windows that I can remember, one faced north and the other one faced south. Its furnishings consisted of a bed, a chair, a chest of drawers, and an old sewing machine. The sewing machine was an old, heavy, black, machine, and stenciled on the front was the name "Singer" in gold letters. It was the treadle-style machine where you had to use your foot to gently rock a pedal back and forth in order to operate it. I loved to make the pedal go back and forth. I wasn't sewing anything, since I had no idea how to sew; I was just making the pedal move. Again, it did not take much to entertain me.

One scary memory that I have of Greg and Bill in their bedroom is that one or the other would get absolutely horrendous nose bleeds. Mom could not remember both of them having a nosebleed at the same time. Either Greg or Bill would be in bed and bleeding profusely from the nose. These incidents were very frightening to me. I sometimes thought that they might bleed to death. These bloody affairs were also frightening to Mom. She worked for what seemed like hours in an attempt to get the hemorrhaging under control. She could not recall all that she did to stop the bleeding, but she remembered wadding up a cloth and pressing it against their upper lip. Mom admitted to me that mostly she just panicked, although this was never evident to me. Greg and Bill were plagued with these periodic bouts of bleeding for years. At some point later in their lives, they both had blood vessels in their noses cauterized to prevent future episodes.

And speaking of bloody, scary moments: it was in Greg and Bill's room that I had my very first period. I do not remember what I was doing in there but all of a sudden I felt moist and sticky. I stopped in my tracks and I looked at myself immediately. I was bleeding. It scared me. Mom had never mentioned anything about this happy moment to me. I cried out for her and she came running up the stairs. I showed her what was happening. She hurried to the bathroom and came back with a sanitary napkin and a white elastic belt. The belt was the way in which pads were kept in place in the olden days. The belt was placed around your waist and the pad ends were pulled through silver grippers located on the front and back of the belt. When I was cleaned up and had my pad in place, Mom showed me the "proper" way to discard of my used napkin. She demonstrated how to carefully roll it up and tie the ends together. Then take toilet paper and wrap it around the pad until it was sufficiently hidden and secured. And then toss it in the garbage. She never explained anything else to me!! I guess she thought I was too young to understand.

Believe it or not, the clothes closet in Greg and Bill's bedroom has an interesting story connected to it. One day, Greg somehow managed to lock himself inside and was unable to get out. To this day, I don't know what he was doing in there or why he went in and locked the door. Mom and Dad tried feverishly for what seemed like an eternity to unlock the door but to no avail. At this point, I think that everyone concerned began to panic. Greg was crying, Dad was mad, and Mom was attempting to orchestrate Greg's escape from solitary confinement. Finally, Dad came to the conclusion that they were getting nowhere fast, so he decided to remove the hinges and take the door off of its frame. Greg was free at last never to pull this stunt again.

The last room on the second floor was the larger of the two bedrooms. The room had two windows that faced west towards Grandma's house. I slept on one side of the room next to the windows, and Mom and Dad slept on the other side of the room. A chest of drawers against the wall acted as a divider. It's funny, although this was Mom and Dad's bedroom, I rarely remember them being in there. I guess I went to sleep long before they did, and they were usually up before me in order to get ready for the day.

One humorous thing concerning my bedroom occurred one night after I went to bed. Mom and Dad remained up entertaining their guests, Dot and Gib Price. It must have been very late, when suddenly I fell out of my bed and hit the floor with what must have been a huge thud. Obviously, I woke up upon impact. But, I simply put myself into bed again. It was no big deal to me. All at once, I heard thunderous footsteps running up the stairs and I was aware of adult voices all around me. I cannot remember their exact words, but I am sure they were wondering whether or not they really heard a loud noise, and if they did, what was it?

Another eye-opening occurrence happened in this bedroom when the aforementioned guests stayed overnight. We did not have guest accommodations, so when Dot and Gib stayed overnight, Dot slept in my bed with me and Gib slept with Mom and Dad in the other bed. It was the crack of dawn and I had just awakened. All of the adults were still asleep. I looked over at Mom, Dad and Gib sleeping in the other bed and there, protruding straight up in the air was Gib's great big penis. My eyes turned into large saucers! I stared at it for what seemed like an eternity. It was big, brown and kind of lumpy-looking; I had never seen anything like it! As a young child, I am not sure if I knew what I was looking at that morning.

Besides the beds and chest of drawers, this room had my little vanity where I worked on my unruly curly hair. The room had a bentwood rocker and a small wooden bookcase located near the north-facing door that led to Greg and Bill's room. At the foot of my bed was my little double-decker baby crib where I kept my stuffed animals and dolls. There was another door that faced east which led to another hallway. There was also a clothes closet in this room where I only remember my little girl clothes hanging. I don't know where Mom and Dad kept their clothes. I think they made a lot of compromises and improvised for their children.

If one turned right at the top of the stairs, you would walk into a long dark, dead-end hallway and Mom and Dad's bedroom was through a door on the right. Behind the far walls of this dark hallway was the apartment of Uncle Bob and his family. There was a locked door (which was never opened) on the left at the end of the hallway that entered into Uncle Bob and Aunt Jane's bedroom. The entire second floor was designed such that you could walk through a series of rooms and doors in a circular pattern and return back to the point of origin --- the top of the stairs.

A final thought concerning my bedroom: for a long time I wanted to have our bedroom painted a beautiful shade of lavender. I also wanted a purple rug. I envisioned the walls lined all around the bottom with pillows. I don't know how or why I came up with this idea but it was all that I could think about. So after much badgering, Mom and Dad relented and painted the bedroom walls a light shade of lavender and bought a purple nylon rug. The pillow idea never materialized though! Upon completion, I thought the room was absolutely beautiful. And amazing as it sounds, that purple rug was in Mom's bedroom in Catonsville and was on the floor till the day she died in 2000.

Well, that was my house. I have tried to remember how it looked, but it is difficult to remember all of the details --- it was a long time ago.

CHAPTER 9

MY GRANTSVILLE RELATIVES

I have already introduced my Uncle Bob, my Mother's brother, in an earlier chapter. I love my Uncle Bob. He is an absolutely wonderful man and has one of the best personalities of anybody I know. One of the best parts of his character is his quick wit. He always has a happy face with a warm smile.

Uncle Bob was married to my Aunt Jane, who I previously mentioned attending our clubhouse plays. Just a few words about Aunt Jane are germane. Jane Davis, nee Hummel, was a neat lady, at least that was my "little girl" perception of her. She always came to our clubhouse skits. She actually laughed and seemed to enjoy them. I thought she was pretty. She was rather petite and walked very fast. She had dark hair, dimples when she smiled, and a nice figure. Her fingernails were long and always nicely manicured.

Aunt Jane

Uncle Bob and Aunt Jane were married in Gainesville, Texas, in 1942. They had two children: Bobbi Jane was born June 1, 1944, and Norman Daniel (Danny) was born February 24, 1948. I think that both children look like Aunt Jane --- especially Bobbi. Their personalities are a blend of Uncle Bob's and Aunt Jane's. Both Danny and Bobbi are friendly, outgoing, affable, and have a quick smile and laugh often.

Most people have a "behind the scenes" personality and I do not know what Jane was like to live with or what sort of partner she was to Bob. I never saw her "other side," but she was always very kind to me and this is how I remember her. She died of Hodgkin's disease in September of 1966. She is buried in the Grantsville Cemetery near the Davis family plot. Many years later, while I was working on the museum in Grantsville, I had the opportunity to meet one of Aunt Jane's brothers. He looked at me and said, "She died much too young."

As I have already mentioned and will continue to mention throughout this book, Danny was a big part of my early childhood. He was always by my side just like Greg and Bill. Danny was actually the "leader" of our small group perhaps because he was the oldest. He was always outside before we were and he would whistle loudly for us to come out and join him. Although, over the years, we have gone our separate ways and have grown apart, he is still very special to me and has a dominant place in my heart and in my early childhood memories. Danny is a great guy!

Although Bobbi Jane was a part of my childhood in Grantsville, she played a much smaller role. Like Andy, I was never very close to her and I think that the reason for this was simply our age difference. I only remember Bobbi as a teenager in Grantsville. She had her own set of friends and her own life apart from mine. Like Aunt Jane, I always thought that Bobbi Jane was so pretty and friendly. She laughed easily and had a bubbly, gregarious personality. I never saw her angry.

Bobbi Jane   **Danny**

In July of 1967, Uncle Bob married Pearl McKenzie, nee Hardesty. Previously, Pearl had been married to Joney McKenzie and they had three children: Pat, Jim, and Terry. You will hear more about Terry in a later chapter, because she was one of my girlfriends in Grantsville. I never knew Pearl very well in Grantsville. I saw her occasionally when I visited Terry, but that was about the extent of our relationship. Of course, I have come to know her better since then. She is a very nice person and I think that she and Bob are a great match. Uncle Bob and Pearl were wonderful to Mom over the years and for this I am grateful. They visited her many times, and they stayed in her home often after the death of Dad.

Uncle Bob and Pearl

Like Pearl, Uncle Bob was not an integral part of my young life in Grantsville either and I think that there may have been two reasons for this. The first reason was my Dad. For a brief period, Dad and Uncle Bob worked together operating the grocery/hardware store. But, as previously mentioned, they had a "falling out." My impression was that Dad and Uncle Bob were never "bosom buddies" and this situation may only have widened the distance between them. However, a discussion with Mom revealed that she felt that the falling out was probably due to Dad's "attitude" about everything and everyone. As a result of this family discord, Uncle Bob didn't come to our house very often, if at all. Second, I think that he was extremely busy running the Davis Hardware Store. These are two excellent reasons why Uncle Bob was not around that often. Plus, I was just a little girl, and Bob and Pearl had their own lives and families and issues.

As years passed, Dad and Uncle Bob seemed to get along better --- at least outwardly. Perhaps they both accepted each other for who they were. I also think that individuals mellow with age and what was once important seems to fade with the passing of time. Just look at the Hatfields and McCoys! They held a grand reunion celebrating a truce to their long embattled family history.

Uncle Bob and Pearl moved from Maryland to Florida and then to Medford, Oregon for a few years. Recently, they relocated to Wilmington, Delaware, where they live in a retirement community. My cousin, Dan Davis lives on Treasure Island due west of Tampa, Florida. Bobbi Jane and her husband live in Huachuca City, Arizona. Pearl's son, Jim McKenzie, lives in Medford, Oregon. Pat McKenzie continues to live in Grantsville. Terry lives near Wilmington in Hockessin, Delaware.

CHAPTER 10

THE SEASONS: FALL AND WINTER

Oh boy! First grade, I was six years old and stood 3' 8½" tall. My favorite song was "Davy Crockett," my favorite color was red, my favorite movie actor was Jerry Mahoney (Paul Winchell's wooden companion), my favorite TV show was "Disneyland," and, of course, my favorite food was corn! My first grade teacher was Mrs. Hughes. I loved Mrs. Hughes. She was short, plump, gray-haired, with a quick smile and a round red nose. She was very kind to all of her students.

Fall always marked the beginning of a new school year. Mom walked with me down to the Grantsville Elementary School each morning, at least for a short while at the start of the first grade. I can't remember all of the specifics of elementary school but certain events do stand out.

I can recall being "in love" with a boy named John Stanton. He had a million freckles and thick brown, wavy hair. I couldn't wait until Valentine's Day to get a card from him. My second great crush was David Wilt and I also had a "thing" for his older brother. In a true oxymoron statement, they were the cute robust "Wilts." Besides all of the puppy love stuff, I can recall the painstaking struggle of learning how to write by making big, neat, perfect block letters between thin blue lines. My ability to read all began with the "Dick and Jane" series of books. My singing career blossomed with the song "Incy, Wincy, Spider." OK, I know what you're thinking, what singing career?

In addition to all of the "normal" things that happened to me in elementary school, I had two physical occurrences that I believe had a somewhat negative effect upon my young, burgeoning self-esteem.

In a first grade picture, I had beautiful, straight, brown hair --- the operative word is "straight." Somewhere between the first and sixth or seventh grade, I must have been abducted by aliens and strange experiments were performed on me. One lasting effect (that I know of) was curly, or should I say kinky hair! My follicles were forever furled. I am kidding of course, I think it was just a delayed, genetic happening --- some weird gene on my Dad's side decided to finally "kick-in".

One quick hair story --- I recall one winter evening it was starting to turn dark, but it really wasn't very late yet. Mom gave me a ten-dollar bill and sent me down the street to Dot McCurdy's hair salon to get my hair trimmed. I went to the salon and got my hair-cut. I was about to pay when I realized my ten-dollar bill was gone! I looked through all of my clothes and in my pockets. At this point, even Dot McCurdy was getting upset. We both decided that I dropped the money in the snow on the way down Main Street. So we went outside in the cold and began retracing my steps. The money must have blown away or it was picked up by someone; I never found it. I felt terrible because I knew we weren't wealthy people and to lose ten dollars was a lot of money. I don't remember how I eventually paid for my hair-cut either.

I have always disliked my hair. I have learned how to work with it after all of these years and make it look fairly nice, especially on low humidity days, but it has certainly been a struggle, especially during my younger, more sensitive years. Today, I will put it up and forget about it --- sort of.

Another physical thing that happened to me during grade school was that I had to start wearing glasses. An optometrist came to the school and discovered that I was not seeing as well as I should have been. I remember my first pair of glasses was shiny, light blue, and metallic. So, here's the picture: I was skinny with frizzy brown hair, shiny blue metallic glasses, freckles, and funny looking teeth which displayed a prominent gap in front. I was quite the looker. Just a note: this gap was "fixed" in 1981, by a dentist named Dr. Pull (no joke).

The outstanding memory I have of my first pair of glasses was the very first time I put them on. I had just come home with my new spectacles and decided to try them out and take a walk around the back yard. To my dismay the glasses made the yard appear as though there were hundreds of small round hills to step over. I must have looked like I had been drinking. I was walking with large, exaggerated steps in an attempt to maneuver over all of the perceived mounds of grass. I eventually became accustomed to my new "eyes" and did in fact see much better.

Some variation of glasses or contacts was a constant aid to my eyes for decades. On February 17, 1998, I had laser vision (Lasik) surgery performed and I am finally able to see without glasses or contact lenses for the first time since grade school! This is a true miracle for me since

I was considered legally blind without the aid of glasses or contact lenses.

Alice in New Blue Metallic Glasses

The kids in my elementary school all seemed to be from poor families. I don't think anybody had much money back then, especially in western Maryland. But, I vividly remember one girl in my class. For some reason, I still think about her and how she looked. It was shocking to me.

Her clothes were filthy and had holes and tears in them. They hung off of her thin body like dirty, old discarded rags. The skin on her face, arms, and legs always had smudges of grime and dirt. Her shoes were worn out and appeared as though they had been handed down in the family from one child to another. They never had laces in them. Her straight, light brown hair was stringy and looked like it hadn't been washed in months. Her long bangs were constantly in her eyes.

I also knew where she lived, a few miles east of Grantsville along Route 40. The house, if you could call it that, was a falling down old, shack. It looked as though this structure would collapse at any moment and fall down over the hillside on which it was precariously balanced so close to the edge. That farm house is no longer occupied, but it is still a junky dilapidated eyesore.

My classmate always looked extraordinarily sad to me. I guess she had good reason to be so forlorn. Who knows what kind of existence she must have had to endure. And yet, even though she appeared so melancholy, there shone through her a kindness and softness that I will never forget. She had the gentlest most sincere face of just about anybody I have ever known. Her large brown eyes were of a person of true grace and tenderness. This aura that she emitted is the essence of why I cannot forget her. I am astonished that an individual like her could have such a profound, long-lasting effect upon me. We really do not know what impact we will have on people that we meet as we travel through our lives. I sometimes wonder where she is now and how the rest of her life unfolded.

In either the second or third grade, I ran head long into another memorable teacher --- the meanest teacher I ever had; I was not only afraid of her, but I hated her as well. She was tall, thin, long-waisted, and had curly brown hair. She had an unattractive horse-like face in that it was rather long and she had a large, lumpy nose. Above her upper lip at one corner of her mouth was a large protruding, flesh-colored mole. Her lips were thick and her mouth was punctuated on either side by deeply grooved lines. She also had huge, bony hands. Her fingers looked like tree frog appendages. They were very long and had rounded tips like suction cups. You know the saying: "Beauty is only skin deep, but ugly goes clear to the bone." This teacher's "ugly" went to the marrow. She was ugly and mean!

One day in class, I am not sure what we were being taught, but I think that it was how to tell time, and for some reason, I simply could not grasp the concept. Miss Meanandugly got positively furious with me. She made me stay after class for what seemed like an eternity. She yelled at me and stormed around the room waving her hands. I don't remember what I had to do to get back into her good graces, but I do remember I was scared to death and indeed, I think that this event traumatized me. I was just a little girl. I later learned that she humiliated Danny by spanking him in front of the class several times.

Mom and Dad later worked with me, and eventually, after many exasperating hours and days, I did learn how to tell time. I think that in today's school environment, Miss Meanandugly would have been reprimanded for acting as she did, but I'm sure nothing happened to her. She probably continued to terrorize young children for many years long after my departure from her classroom. One truly amazing fact to this story was that this teacher had a sister, who also taught at the Grantsville Elementary School. She was very attractive and nice. It was hard to believe that they were sisters. Miss Meanandugly has since passed away, but my memories of her will live on forever.

After grade school, I began attending junior high school at Northern High School located near Accident, about 15 miles southwest of Grantsville. However, when you are riding on a large, lumbering school bus full of noisy kids, it seemed like a 60-mile ride each way, everyday! Junior high was somewhat uneventful for me.

I remember one teacher that I had for basic math. What a dull, uninspiring individual! Even his name was boring: Mr. Brown. I never learned much in his class. If I had had an interesting, exciting instructor for math early in my educational career, I could have done much better in this area. I have certainly learned much about math since then. Actually I am pretty good with math, but I think that I could have excelled in this subject. I am always thrilled when my checkbook balances.

Trying out for cheerleader was one final traumatic event that occurred during my junior high school experience in western Maryland. What a devastating event! I was so nervous. I tried very hard to do all of the acrobatics and routines required to make the team, but in the end, they did not call my name. I think the main reason that I was not selected was that I wasn't cute enough. I still had my kinky, now pulled-back hair, glasses, freckles, and a gap-toothed smile.

Of course, Terry Jo McKenzie made the Cheerleading Squad, but she was really pretty. I was always just a little bit jealous of her. Terry, the youngest daughter of Pearl and Joney McKenzie, also grew up in Grantsville, and we hung around with each other quite a bit. We are the same age, in fact only a few days separate our August birthdays.

Following my failure to become a cheerleader, I decided that perhaps I could become a majorette. However, in order to become a majorette, one has to learn how to twirl a baton! An integral part of baton twirling is throwing this slim, silver, whirling piece of metal high into the air and then catching it. I tried, but I was always so nervous about being bashed in the head or having my nose broken by my usually out of control baton that I never became a majorette either.

Alice eyeing Terry

Terry always seemed to get the cute guys and other girls emulated her style. One time Terry had just gotten an extremely tight, curly permanent and she looked really cute. Of course, Terry could have shaved her head and still looked good. There was a girl who was in the school band with Terry and me, and she showed up the very next day with the exact same tightly curled coiffure. She was a rather homely girl to begin with, but when she arrived for band practice with this hairdo, she looked even homelier. Her skin was very pale, she was quite thin and small, and she had an enormous nose with several obvious bumps. She looked like the last of the poodle litter that nobody wanted and had been left at the pound. She looked absolutely absurd. I am certain that she heard the kids laughing at her.

I never enjoyed school: elementary, junior, or high school. I sometimes wonder if Miss Meanandugly was the "defining moment" for me in terms of disliking school. I never excelled in the learning process except for an occasional class here and there over the years. I gravitated towards generalized studies or non-academic, vocational-type classes, such as secretarial or home economics courses. I felt like such a dud --- like the black sheep of the family. My parents and brothers all did well in school and obtained college degrees. It was not until I was much older and attending George Mason University that I began to realize how important and exciting an education can be. I finally received my college degree in May of 1993, and I realized that I was not so "dumb" after all --- I graduated with a 3.84 overall grade point average (GPA) and a 4.00 GPA in my major.

Fall is an absolutely beautiful time of the year in western Maryland. The cool, sometimes frigid nights and wonderfully warm days turn the leaves breathtaking shades of red, yellow, and orange. Because we attended school during the week and it turned dark relatively early during this time of the year, we stuck pretty close to home. But weekends were another story. Danny was always the first one up. He would stand outside of our house and whistle shrilly. This was our wake up call. I think that we were up, dressed, and out of the door within 15 minutes of his summons. I am not sure if we even ate breakfast or brushed our teeth. We were so anxious to get our exciting day started. Of course, being whistled awake happened on a daily basis during the summer months.

On weekends during the school year, we were outside most of the day, if the weather was decent. Usually we rode our bikes, especially on warm fall days. The cool, crisp fall mornings motivated many of our road adventures. I remember one day late in the year that Danny, Greg, Bill and I decided to take a long bike ride. I don't remember where we traveled that day, probably over to Pennsylvania somewhere, but we were gone all day, from early in the morning until after dark. When we got back, all the parents were hopping mad. The fact that we were gone for such a long time was unusual, even for the fearsome foursome. I don't recall how my brothers and I were disciplined, but I am sure we were told, "Never to do that again!" Poor Danny received the worst of the punishment, since he was the oldest and considered the "ring leader." He received the "belt" a few times from his Dad.

Danny recalled one road trip event of which I had long forgotten. On one long and grueling bike trip, Greg and Bill got so tired they could not go on. So Danny rode back to get Greg, put him on his handle bars and carried him to a certain point, probably to the top of a hill; then he went back to get Bill, and did the same thing. I guess Danny also walked Greg and Bill's bikes up the hill one at a time, too.

In another exciting misadventure, Danny, Greg, Bill and I decided that we should explore an old excavation pit located just east of town. It was a steep drop over the bank, and we were walking around the edge when suddenly Bill slipped and tumbled down the rocky slope, perhaps 12 or 15 feet. He hit the back of his head on a rock causing a one-inch bloody gash. Dan sprang into action and rushed Bill by bike back to town. Greg and I followed close behind. We were all nervous about getting into trouble, so Dan took him up to his house (no one was home). There, Dan cleaned the head wound as best he could, and then sent Bill home. I guess we got away with this caper, because we never heard a word from any of the parents.

As children, we were very rarely punished physically. I may have been spanked one or two times at most. I remember that Mom slapped me across the face once because I tore a brand new blouse --- we had just brought it home from a shopping trip to Meyersdale and I decided to try it on. It was a long, white cotton blouse decorated with tiny brown giraffes, and a spaghetti strap-like belt that tied in front. For some reason, I was in a hurry to get it off (I probably wanted to go outside and play) and as I struggled to remove it, the entire seam along one side ripped apart. Being slapped was quite a surprise and it also hurt my feelings, but I now understand Mom's anger.

I honestly don't believe that we gave Mom and Dad many reasons to punish us. We were basically pretty good kids. When we did misbehave, such as the bike riding incident, we understood their anger. Verbal reprimands and stern "looks" were sufficient --- we usually did not need to be told a second time.

Fall was a big deal because that was when new cars were showcased at the local Ford Dealership. One might think, "Oh, my God, why not watch the grass grow, too?" But that was life in Grantsville back then. Little things could be quite exciting; things that we take for granted in today's world. Our whole family went down to the showroom to admire the new models. There were balloons, games and hot dogs. It was a carnival-like atmosphere and it was fun for kids.

Even though there were other car dealerships in town, we always went to the Ford Dealership, because Dad was a firm believer in Fords. For many years, he drove a late 1950's Ford Falcon. It was a good little car, but it was painted the funniest looking blue you can imagine. It was a mix between a robin's egg blue and the ugliest turquoise blue eye shadow ever made. Understandably, I have never seen this color on a car since. Dad eventually "totaled" our trusty blue Ford Falcon in front of the Candlelight Inn Restaurant just blocks away from our home in Catonsville. I was told that the brakes failed on the old car.

October meant Halloween! We always had a good time during this holiday. I don't remember many specifics except that Greg, Bill and I would dress up in costumes. We walked from one end to the other end of Grantsville stopping at every house. We returned home after "Trick or Treating" with enormous bags full of all kinds of candy that we would eat for weeks. No wonder I had so many cavities at such a tender young age. We also would sometimes do a few tricks like "soaping" windows. One time we knocked on a crotchety old man's door, then ran away before he could answer. Occasionally, toilet paper unraveled and mysteriously appeared in trees, but, indeed, no felonies were ever committed in the name of Halloween by the Faith kids!

We were fortunate, because back then we never had to worry about razor blades in our candy bars or being abducted by child molesters. Halloween was a carefree, kid-friendly celebration. I am so very thankful that I have this as a part of my happy childhood experiences. Because of these cheerful memories, I still get a little excited about this time of year. I enjoy the scariness of it all.

Fall turns into winter, sometimes much faster than one would like, especially in Garrett County, but there is absolutely nothing like winter in western Maryland. If the Baltimore area receives 3 inches of snow in December, chances are Garrett County will have 3 feet, or more. Although there are now all kinds of winter sports available in Garrett County --- downhill skiing, snowmobiling, cross-country skiing, sleigh rides, tobogganing, and snow boarding. In the 1950's in Grantsville, the biggest sport was SLEDDING.

After a winter storm, there was nothing more thrilling for us than climbing to the top of a hill that was located near the center of town and racing down that hill on our wooden sleds. We would trudge up and fly down this hill over and over for hours on end until way after dark. It would be freezing cold, our faces would be red and frozen numb with our noses running, but we never seemed to notice or care. We started at the very top of this hill, slid down the slope to the bottom of the hill, and continued on until reaching the edge of the icy white lawn. At that point, a sharp right turn was required in order to enter into the back alley. By this time we had gained enough momentum to streak down the alley for many yards. We never had to worry about cars --- there were hardly any on normal, sunny days, and after a snowstorm: what cars? This was great fun.

There were always the occasional snowball fights which I hated as much as our nasty apple fights. For some reason, my brothers, including Andy sometimes, and my cousin Danny, took these fights all too seriously. They all had pretty darn good aim and since I was the only female, I was the target more often than not. Although I participated, snowball fights were not one of my favorite winter past times.

In addition to the snow ball fights, we also created a game called "King of the Mountain." Every winter after several large snow storms a gigantic mountain of snow appeared on the side road which led to the back alley. I don't think that we ever wondered how the mountain of snow got there; we were just excited to have the opportunity to play our game again. All of us kids would climb to the top of the mountain of white stuff. Of course, "climbing" to the top was pretty tough. Enough time had elapsed that the snow had become compacted and was very slippery. After finally reaching the top or some area close to the top, we tried to push each other down the mountain. The last kid "standing" (or clinging desperately) nearest to the top was "King of the Mountain."

Due to its high elevation --- 3,360 feet at the highest point on Backbone Mountain --- and relatively cold climate, Garrett County can have enormous snowstorms. During the great blizzard of 1918, Army soldiers were brought in to shovel open the roads. During another blizzard in 1920, an estimated four to five hundred automobiles were stranded along the National Road between Grantsville and Uniontown, Pennsylvania, a section of road only 30 miles long. There have been many catastrophic snow storms since then.

Try to imagine our backyard in Grantsville after one of these cold, wintry, white assaults by Mother Nature. After you have pictured our backyard covered with snow, then visualize very deep snow, maybe seven or eight feet high, then finally envision me as a three or four foot tall, skinny little girl in the middle of all of this white stuff. The snow would sometimes be two or three feet over our heads. Scooping out passageways in the snow seemed like the natural thing to do. We excavated long narrow paths through the snow, creating quite a maze. I am glad that we never had any cave-ins with all of that snow piled up around us. We would run along the slippery, high-walled trails and hide from each other. We had great fun.

One winter day I walked up to Terry's house to play with her. She lived at the far west end of Grantsville. We were enjoying ourselves doing whatever we were doing, when all of a sudden we decided that I should stay overnight. This was so important to us that we decided to pray. Terry was Catholic, so she pulled out her Bible and her rosary beads, and we knelt down on our knees and prayed for hours in her bedroom.

This was my first time at performing such an ordeal. My knees ached by the end of the day.

I picked up the phone at Terry's house around 5:00 p.m. and I called Mom to ask if I could stay overnight with Terry. I was so nervous --- I was sure she was going to say "No." But, all of that praying paid off! I was shocked when she said "OK." We were ecstatic! I don't remember what I did for pajamas; I must have borrowed a pair of Terry's. We had already gone to bed, but we were not yet asleep. It was around 11:00 p.m., when I decided that I was hungry. I asked Terry if she had anything to eat in the house. She said yes, so we tip-toed downstairs. I was hoping for a sandwich or something substantial. She opened the cupboard and took out a big jar of peanut butter and then she took out a large spoon from a silverware drawer. That was it --- a big spoonful of peanut butter! I guess I should have started praying again for food.

I was so disappointed that I wanted to go home immediately. I called Mom and Dad to come and get me. For some reason, I thought that they would drive the car up to Terry's, but about 45 minutes later there was knock on the door and there were Mom and Dad --- they walked up in the cold, winter evening. I also thought that they would be furious with me, but surprisingly, they were not angry at all. As a matter of fact, I think that they rather enjoyed their long walk up to Terry's in the bright moonlight through the sparkling snow. We walked back home, but I ran slightly ahead, anxious to return home. Mom may have even made some of her delicious hot cocoa when we got home that evening. Terry probably never forgave me for running out on her, but we never discussed it again. Afterward, I was somewhat disappointed in myself for acting like I did.

As you have probably already discerned, dancing was a big part of my early teen years. I absolutely loved to dance and I was good at it. In addition to dancing at the American Legion nearly every Friday night, a group of us would travel occasionally to Frostburg, Maryland, a larger town about 15 miles east of Grantsville. Every Saturday night, there was a dance held at a place called the "Chatter Box." Since we were dependent on an adult driving us to Frostburg, we were unable to go very often. Usually, Jimmy McKenzie, Terry's older brother, would drive us to Frostburg and then pick us up later to go home.

The "Chatter Box" was located on Main Street and was not very big. As a result, it was wall-to-wall kids, and sometimes it was nearly impossible to do our new Jitterbug "moves." The American Legion and the "Chatter Box" were the places where I honed my skill as a dancer. Several years later, after our move to Catonsville, I auditioned and was selected as a dancer to appear on a local Baltimore television dance show similar to American Bandstand.

As a side note, one evening in 1959, Elvis Presley and his entourage made a surprise stop at Robertson's Restaurant (now the Wildwater Inn, a local "watering hole") located on Route 40 a few miles east of Grantsville. Little did I know, but many times while traveling to and from the Chatter Box, we drove right by this roadside restaurant. However, I heard later a number of local kids went there to see Elvis, but he was already gone. I missed out on this notable event, but I was only 10 years old, so I probably would not have rushed down to see him anyway. Apparently, Elvis was traveling across country by car when they stopped to eat at this roadside restaurant. One can only imagine the stunned silence of those patrons inside that evening.

A chapter on winter would not be complete without mentioning Christmas in Grantsville. I loved Christmas because Mom and Dad knocked themselves out to make it a special time of year. We always seemed to find the tallest (high as the ceiling), most beautiful pine trees. Mom preferred short-needled conifers, so that's what we bought every year. We positioned the tree in one corner of the living room and secured it with a piece of string tied to a nail which Dad had pounded into the wall. This nail was never removed and probably remained in the wall long after we moved out.

The family had so much fun decorating our enormous tree. Mom pulled out boxes and boxes of carefully wrapped decorations from a large cardboard container. Each box was tied with white cotton string which was carefully untied and placed on the lid which in turn was tucked underneath the box. I guess we did this so that the string was not lost. There was certainly a "fine science" involved in packing and unpacking Christmas decorations. I find myself following the exact same routine as an adult. It is amazing what habits stay with you throughout life.

We spent hours gently placing a large array of brightly colored balls and other ornaments on the tree. Occasionally, we would have to search for a lost or missing hook. Surprisingly, very few ornaments got broken. There were festive little pine cones, and tiny colorful moons with a man's face on it --- the "Man in the Moon." There were fancy peacocks with long plastic tail feathers that clamped onto the branches. The colorful variety of ornaments made the tree not only beautiful, but interesting to look at as well.

The last thing that we added to the tree, were long, shimmering strands of silver tinsel. The placement of the tinsel had to be just right or it would look uneven and funny. Also, the strands could not be hung in clumps, but had to be delicately draped on the tree branch two or three at a time. I think that our tinsel hanging scenes would have made a great episode for the Jerry Seinfeld Show. Done. Gorgeous.

Our Beautiful Christmas Tree

Christmas morning in the Faith household can only be described as chaotic exhilaration bordering on spontaneous combustion --- I was sure that I would explode with excitement. It was all I could do to get any sleep on Christmas Eve. My brothers and I would get up at the crack of dawn, tumble over each other to get down the stairs, and tear into the huge pile of presents which Santa had left. All this time we would be laughing and squealing. We were fortunate to receive so many wonderful gifts. Invariably, we received everything that we asked Santa to bring.

I recall one Christmas specifically asking for a Ballerina Doll. That was all I really wanted that year. I opened what I thought was my last present and I was so disappointed when there was no doll. I ran upstairs, woke Mom up and said, "Mom, Mom, Santa didn't bring me my Ballerina Doll!" She replied: "Go look again." I ran back downstairs and looked again. Sure enough, tucked behind the tree to one side was another present. It was my Ballerina Doll!

I did not realize until much later in my adult life, how hard Mom and Dad worked to make Christmas special for us kids. They must have been up most of the night, wrapping all of the presents. I don't know when they found the time, where they went to purchase these unique gifts, and where they hid all of them for probably weeks if not months. My parents certainly used stealth-like maneuvers to create the perfect Christmas. Thank you, Mom and Dad for making Christmas so special for our family. Christmas will always remain in my heart as a very magical time.

We entertained ourselves inside when the winter weather was bad. One favorite activity was playing with our rather extensive train set. We set it up in Greg and Bill's bedroom. The train had to pass underneath the bed because there wasn't much room. We had all kinds of little houses, trees, railroad signs, and other landscape paraphernalia. It took us hours to set things up, and we would leave it in place for days.

We played with this same train set in the house that we rented in Catonsville. We set it up in a back bedroom that had a door to the outside. We worried about burglars because one time we heard someone jiggling that particular doorknob. Dad even went around the house after this incident and nailed all of the windows shut! Anyway, it was a running joke that if a burglar ever broke in, they would probably create such an enormous racket stumbling over the train set that they would surely be scared off.

Another activity that we did indoors was play with marbles. We had lots of marbles of all sizes, designs and colors that we rolled down a brown, wooden zigzag contraption. I am not sure what the point was --- I think we just enjoyed the movement and the noise they made hitting the end at each level and rolling back and forth down the little shoots.

Another pastime that we had was playing with buttons. Yes, I said buttons. Mom had a big box of buttons of all kinds --- fancy ones, plain ones, big ones, small ones, unusual looking ones, you name it. Anyway, Greg, Bill and I spent hours playing with these buttons. We invented all kinds of games. As I have said already, it did not take much to entertain us!

Yes, winter could be harsh in Grantsville, but I welcomed this season each year with great anticipation, excitement and joy.

CHAPTER 11

THE SEASONS: SPRING AND SUMMER

Ahh, springtime, and a young girl's fancy turns to a dog. It was sometime during late spring. School was still in session, and I was walking along the back alley towards home when I suddenly came upon the cutest puppy eating the berries off of a currant bush. He must have been starved because he looked very skinny. Of course, I had to stop to talk to him and pet him. He was the sweetest little dog. He was mostly black and brown, but he had small patches of white fur, too. A veterinarian later identified him as a Sheltie Collie mix, but we will never know what breeds made up the mix. As we came to appreciate Shag, we came to the realization that his father was probably pretty wild.

Shag

I began to walk home and the puppy followed me. I was certain that Mom and Dad would never let me keep him, so I did everything I could think of to shoo him away. I kept telling him to "go away" and stomped my feet, but to no avail. I began to run, but he ran too, following me all the way home. I just could not shake the little fellow.

I was afraid to take him into my house, so I headed for Grandma's house. Andy was the mastermind behind this caper. He decided that we should hide the dog behind one of Grandma's couches in the living room. I don't think that the puppy peed on anything back there; at least there was no lingering smell. Believe me, Grandma's nose would have detected it and we would have heard about it! It would have been a "balls in the stomach" moment. I cannot recall Grandma's reaction or that of my parents for that matter, but the puppy stayed. Soon we were all sitting around trying to come up with an appropriate name for our shaggy, little stray. Andy threw out the name "Shag" and it stuck for nearly 18 years.

Shag was quite old when he died. It was one of my brothers who first noticed him lying under a tree outside of our home in Catonsville and hurried inside to tell Mom. She tried to help Shag by wringing water from a wet rag into his mouth. He must have been in pretty bad shape at this point. My parents carefully placed him in a large box and rushed him to a local veterinarian, but it was too late. He'd had a stroke. Mom was devastated at the loss of Shag.

I was living overseas when Shag died. It was not until I came home for a visit that I learned he had died. I was standing in the kitchen talking to Mom, when I backed up and instinctively I moved to avoid Shag's food and water bowl. I looked down and the bowls were gone. It was then that I knew.

Shag was an independent dog. He did his own thing. I remember one evening in 1968, during my wedding reception (my first wedding) at Mom and Dad's house in Catonsville. There were small hors d'oeuvres sitting on a coffee table in the living room. I happened to look over, and there was Shag eyeing the platter. He very delicately cocked his head to one side, and then carefully and deliberately selected one item from near the corner of the table. He did not disturb anything else on the table, and did not return for more. He was quite intelligent.

There was a wild streak in this gentle dog. He would run away from home and be gone for days, but he always returned. Mom and Dad had to rescue him from the pound on more than one occasion during mating season. The true collie "mix" came out in Shag many times, for he loved to run free. At the same time, he remained steadfastly loyal to his masters --- the Faith Family --- for many years.

Mom owned pets throughout her life. After the loss of Shag, Mom acquired a female miniature Schnauzer and named her Tessie. Tess was a great little dog. Mom had her for many years until she, too, succumbed to what appeared to be a stroke. Soon after Tessie was put to sleep, Mom was fortunate enough to spot a newspaper advertisement selling miniature Schnauzers. Mom and a friend hopped in the car and drove over to see the dogs. Mom could not resist them and came home with two puppies, a brother and sister. She named them George and Dolly. In addition to all of these canines, Mom had at least two birds, and a cat named Annie B. I am glad that Mom had her pets over the years. I think that they kept her young at heart, vital, and gave her a reason to get up every morning. I am certain that they not only added life to her years, but years to her life.

Dandelions! Dandelions! Just outside of Grandma's back porch door was a cement stoop surrounded by a wire fence with tiny openings just the right size for a dandelion stem. Greg, Bill and I would spend hours picking dandelions from Grandma's backyard and sticking their fragile, milk-dripping stems into these little holes until we filled every last one and there were hundreds. Our fingers would be sticky, stained, and smelly from the white liquid. The finished product looked pretty good, worthy of a picture perhaps. But the beauty did not last very long. The flowers would begin to droop within hours of the finished masterpiece. We performed this tedious task over and over again until the dandelions' bright yellow "hair" turned gray and flew away.

At times we were pretty sadistic. It was during late spring that nasty looking caterpillars would appear in the yard. I hated the brown, squirmy, fuzzy, little buggers. I guess Greg and Bill did too, because we conspired to collect them in our little red wagon and performed periodic mass murders. We gathered up hundreds of caterpillars at one time and proceeded to pour boiling hot water on them. The trick was keeping them from crawling out while we boiled the water. We would also occasionally hold a large magnifying glass over their little bodies focusing the sunlight until they started to smoke and burn! How sick was that? I cannot remember what we did with their little carcasses. I hope that PETA (People for the Ethical Treatment of Animals) members never read this chapter. I could never do this to any living creature today, not even a creepy crawly caterpillar.

Spring in Grantsville meant a visit from the Easter Bunny. Mom and Dad made Easter an extraordinary event for us kids each year. Coloring Easter eggs was so much fun. Mom bought Paz egg coloring kits that contained all of the necessary paraphernalia to dye Easter eggs. Lord knows we didn't need to purchase the EGGS. Each kit contained: six or so dye pills of various colors, a copper wire egg holder, a wax pencil, and a variety of decals which we could "tattoo" onto our colored eggs. Mom spread out newspapers to cover our kitchen table and boiled water. She then filled coffee cups with hot water, adding just the right amount of vinegar to help set the dyes. To this day, when I smell vinegar, I think of coloring Easter eggs.

Now it was our turn. We dropped in the dye pill of our color choice. Sometimes we experimented and mixed two different colored pills together creating some pretty terrible looking eggs, but each completed egg was beautiful to its creator. After being dyed, each egg was carefully placed on the newspaper to dry. Sometimes we would blow on it to speed up the drying process. After it dried, we sometimes applied a decal --- we left some of the eggs plain. Applying a decal involved cutting out one of the many images that were included in the kit and placing it face down on the egg. Then a warm, wet cloth was placed on top of the picture for a few seconds, and "voila," you had an egg with an image on it. We could also use the wax pencil to write messages on the egg before beginning the coloring process --- the waxed area of the egg remained color-free. I didn't use the pencil very often. We colored dozens of hard-boiled eggs and had such a wonderful time in the process. It was truly a fun family event.

Our job was coloring the eggs but Mom's was assembling the Easter baskets. Although Mom occasionally used "real" woven baskets, she routinely used "recycled" cartons that she collected, like old cottage cheese containers or something similar. Into each "basket," Mom placed green Easter "grass," chocolate bunnies, jelly beans, yellow or pink marshmallow "peeps," toys, other goodies, and of course, our rainbow assortment of newly colored Easter eggs. Then when we kids were out of sight, she placed them in hiding places in the backyard. For years, she hid them in fairly easy places so they would all be found, but as we got older and wiser, she began placing the baskets in extremely weird and hard to find places. I am certain that an Easter basket still waits to be discovered somewhere in Grandma's backyard! Searching out these baskets of goodies was great fun for us, and I think Mom enjoyed making them up and then hiding them.

Summers in Grantsville were spent almost entirely outdoors. We kids only came inside the house to eat, sleep, or use the bathroom. We enjoyed so many different activities: from badminton, to croquet, to just running around in the rain during a shower. We were perpetual motion.

But before telling you about all of the fun we had, I should mention a couple of tragedies --- at least they seemed like tragedies to us at the time. One beautiful summer day, I decided that it was time to learn how to ride my two-wheeled bicycle. I had been using training wheels, but I was sure that I was beyond such childish necessities. I slowly walked my bike to the top of the hill (I was a little nervous) in Grandma's backyard just next to the large white cherry tree. Down the hill I went. I was doing pretty well --- at least I remained upright, until about mid-way down when I forgot how to apply the brakes and was heading straight for the climbing rosebush. I crashed head long into this thorny obstacle.

What a mess I was with little daggers stuck into my skin from the top of my head all the way down my legs to where my socks stopped --- everywhere there was skin, there were thorns. Everyone gathered around me picking out the thorns. I guess I am extremely lucky that I have only one small scar under my mouth that acts as a permanent reminder of this mishap. Most importantly, however, this didn't stop me from riding my bike. I continued struggling to learn to ride and eventually I became an excellent bike rider.

A second "tragic" event that happened one summer in Grantsville involved Bill. One day he got the urge to go to the bathroom. He was outdoors, so he decided to use an old tin can that he found. Where he got this tin can, I do not know --- tin cans were not a normal part of the landscape in our yard. Whatever the source, he pushed the ragged metal lid downward and began to pee in the convenient container. I assume that he pushed the lid down, because when he began to pull out his penis, the lid clamped down trapping his delicate member. He was stuck. I do not remember what he did next, but eventually Mom came to the rescue, wrapped a big winter coat around him (remember it was summertime), and hauled him off to Dr. Strong, the local doctor. He came home minus one tin can fastened to his penis --- he was lucky that he was not minus one penis!

A final potentially serious injury was endured in the "name of love." I had a crush on a boy who lived in Grantsville. His name was Roger. I don't remember what I had done on this particular day to provoke him perhaps I was teasing him or maybe even throwing rocks at him! Suddenly, he picked up a good-sized rock and threw it at me. I spun away trying to avoid being hit, but the rock struck me in the back of my head. Gosh it hurt. My head was bleeding and I ran into the house. Mom came to my rescue and managed to stop the bleeding. If I remember correctly, Roger came in and apologized to me. I'll never know whether he came under his own volition or if an adult forced him to make amends. Anyway, I quickly gave up on Roger, but still have an annoying little bump on the back of my head as a token of his "affection."

There were other minor wounds inflicted on us kids over the years by mishaps such as the bike wreck where I skidded on the gravel in the back alley and "crashed and burned." I walked away with tiny pieces of grit and stone embedded in my skin and still have a scar on my knee from this accident. I also managed to fall off of a trapeze one summer. The trapeze was a part of the swing set located in front of our house. The fall from my high swinging perch completely knocked the wind out of me. I was sure I had died. It is amazing that none of us ever incurred a broken bone or sustained more serious injuries given how physically active we were.

I have another story involving animals that took place during the summer. Beyond the back alley and behind our barn was a large pasture which was home to a number of Holstein cows. Our family did not own these cows nor did we own the pastureland. But we kids spent many hours roaming around within its borders and I stepped in more than one big, stinky, brown cow paddy. One summer morning while I was walking around in the pasture, I decided to sing to the cows. I guess I thought they would enjoy an early morning serenade. I was wrong. All of a sudden one of the cows charged me. I was sure that I would be trampled to death, but I reached the fence and crawled under it just in the nick-of-time. I was safe but the event really frightened me and I learned my lesson. I never sang to the cows again.

And speaking of cows, adjacent to the pasture, was a large black barn, formerly the blacksmith shop, and an apple orchard. This is the area where we would occasionally have some ferocious apple-throwing fights. There were always bushels of ammunition! As I mentioned earlier, I hated these fruit-fights as much as I disliked snowball throwing battles. I would always be hit with small, round green apple "bullets." This orchard area is also where I remember the electrified cow pasture fence. Sometimes I would touch the wire for just a second in order to get a small shock! How weird is that?

As I mentioned above, we enjoyed a variety of outdoors activities during the summer months. Of course, bike riding was our major preoccupation, but when it got really hot, there was nothing better than slipping and sliding on our bright yellow, plastic "Slip N' Slide." We extended our long yellow plastic slide down the very same hill where I began my disastrous descent into the rosebush. The slide was long, maybe 20 to 30 feet in length and approximately four to five feet wide. A sprinkler system attached to a hose covered the surface with a slippery layer of water. With our bathing suits on, we were ready for action. One by one we started running and took a flying leap onto the plastic, usually landing on our back, and slid to the end. There would sometimes be annoying dry spots that briefly interrupted our downward descent, but overall the ride was great.

Badminton was another summer favorite. Once we got the net set up in the backyard, we played for hours. We enjoyed this game on warm summer nights, and hit the birdie or shuttlecock back and forth with our rackets until darkness began to fall. As a matter of fact, we played for so long that bats joined us for their evening feedings. They flew so fast, low and close to our heads that I was sure they would become entangled in our hair. It was nearly impossible to see them coming.

We also spent many enjoyable hours playing croquet. It took time to set up the necessary wooden stakes and metal wickets to play the game properly; exact placement was paramount. The basic rules of croquet are simple, each player attempts to hit their ball through a series of wickets placed in the grass. The first one to get his or her ball through all of the wickets was the winner. We were quite competitive. Occasionally, it was necessary to whack an opponent's ball out of the way. This was accomplished by placing your ball next to your opponent's, resting your foot on top of your ball, and then hitting your ball with your mallet sending your opponent's ball flying, hopefully far away. Sometimes when I tried this, I missed the ball and hit my foot. Ouch! Grandma's croquet set was so worn from constant use that it was difficult to discern just what color the stripes on a balls and mallets were supposed to be, but we didn't care.

Sometimes being outside in the summertime was a simple thing to do. When the skies turned dark and rain began to fall, we quickly changed into our bathing suits and ran around in the rain for as long as the storm lasted. This was great fun especially at the end of an especially hot, humid day. The raindrops sometimes stung as they pounded down on our skin --- Mother Nature's shower massage. I am sure that Mom kept an eye on the sky for lightning. When the rain stopped and the sun came out again, we shook the branches of each and every tree and tall bush in the yard to create our own mini "rain showers."

Another innocent childhood pastime was catching fireflies in glass jars. During warm summer nights, there were hundreds of lighting bugs darting through the darkness. We ran around for hours in the evening running after them. After we captured enough bugs, we took the jar inside and quickly punched several holes in the lid so that the poor things could breath. But once these fascinating, flying, flickering, living lights were confined to their glass prisons, they lost their appeal and they certainly did not live very long in captivity. Was this activity more of our sadistic nature coming out?

When we needed yet another diversion, we made "tanks" out of discarded cardboard refrigerator boxes. We retrieved these containers from the appliance store adjacent to our house. One end of the box would already be open, and we unfastened the other end creating an enormous, tube. We managed to drag the boxes back to Grandma's back yard where one or two of us would climb in and began to roll the thing across the yard. Sometimes we collided (we could not see where we were going) with an opposing tank and a battle ensued. The battle consisted of each tank ramming one another until one or the other gave up and retreated. Gosh, we had fun!

Occasionally, we put two, three, or even four boxes together creating one long tunnel. Sometimes we became "architects," arranging the boxes at angles to form several rooms much like a small ranch house or mobile home. It became our little "hideout." Many nights we carried our pillows and blankets out to the boxes and slept there. Unfortunately, they were just cardboard boxes and the ground sure got hard! When it rained, we covered the boxes with our Slip N' Slide. Pretty smart, huh? Sadly, the boxes still got pretty soggy and smelly after a summer rain!

One of the most frightening games we played outside was "Three Bears Out Tonight." We may have made it up but in any event, we sure scared ourselves in the process of playing it. The concept was quite simple. One person was selected to be the "monster" and would hide somewhere, anywhere, in the backyard. The remaining children became the "three bears." The three bears would count to a designated number allowing enough time for the "monster" to hide. Once the three bears finished their countdown, they skipped around the yard, all the while singing "Three Bears Out Tonight." The longer and farther the "bears" skipped, the scarier and tenser the game became --- remember, it was also very dark. We never knew where the monster was hiding, but all of a sudden we heard a roar and out would jump the "monster" that ran after us. Of course, we were screaming our heads off by this time, and ran like crazy back to the designated safe area. The "bear" that the "monster" caught would become the next "monster" and this person had to find a new place to hide. Greg, Bill, Danny entertained ourselves for hours playing this simple summer game.

Grantsville did not have a movie theater (and still doesn't), so occasionally, the whole family jumped into the Falcon and drove to the Roxy Theater in Meyersdale. It seemed like a long distance over the winding, curvy mountain roads but Meyersdale was only 13 miles northeast of Grantsville. This was a real thrill for us kids. We very rarely went to the movies. As a matter of fact, the only movies that I remember going to see were: "North to Alaska," "Old Yeller," "The Yearling," and "Darby O'Gill and the Little People." This was the dark ages before Video Cassette Recorders (VCRs) and Blockbuster movie rentals, Showtime, Home Box Office (HBO), Netflix, and the ability to purchase a movie at the grocery story along with your frozen dinners. The only way to see a movie in the 1950's and 1960's was to go to a theater. Movies are so prevalent today; the fun has gone out of "going to the movies" for me. Back then, there was real excitement and anticipation about seeing a movie in a theater. I am glad it was like that back then.

My summer adventures would not be complete without telling you about our family vacations to Ocean City, Maryland. We did not travel to the ocean very often because it was a relatively long car trip for us, especially driving along Route 40 over the mountains of western Maryland. It took seven hours or more to reach our destination. Remember, this was long before Interstate 68 was even in the planning stage. I sometimes wonder if Mom and Dad developed a love for the ocean during the early days of their marriage when they lived on the Eastern Shore.

We did not have a lot of money to spend on a luxurious hotel, and the concept of a Holiday Inn Express was far in the future, so we inevitably stayed at the beautiful "Crystal Motel." I am, of course, being quite facetious. The Crystal Motel could be described in many ways but beautiful is not one of them. It was a plain, small white motel and the word which best describes this one-story motel was "austere." It was not sleazy or dumpy --- it was just very basic with absolutely no frills. Not surprisingly, there always seemed to be a vacancy. The Crystal Motel was located at the edge of the main highway leading into Ocean City, across the busy highway from the ocean. It was not an ideal location for families with young children. We could not just run out of the motel door and dive into the ocean.

We all stayed in one small room --- Dad, Mom, Greg, Bill, and me. I don't recall if Andy ever came along. The room had a cement floor with no carpeting --- like a large prison cell except that there were no bars on the windows. Sand was absolutely everywhere --- all over the floor, in the bed sheets, yuk! It had a tiny bathroom and some penitentiary-like bunk beds. I don't remember where Mom and Dad slept, maybe standing up! One time when we were there, it rained for days. We played board games and perhaps cards on the only table in the room. Mom and Dad came prepared!

When the weather was nice, we played on the beach. I was always attacked by mosquitoes --- they loved me, and they still do. One evening I was running along the beach and a mosquito bit me right on the nose. An enormous, horrible red bump appeared, and I decided that I had had enough of the ocean! Mom and Dad did their best to make our stays at the ocean enjoyable, and for the most part, these vacations were fun. We certainly had a great time splashing around in the cold salty water, collecting seashells, and spending quality time as a family. After all, isn't that what it is all about?

One of my favorite summer activities was something that I still enjoy doing today --- SHOPPING! However, the way I shop today is very different from the way I shopped 50 years ago. Today, I wander aimlessly through the malls in my jeans and flip-flops, sometimes eating a soft pretzel or slurping a Starbucks coffee. Back then, I wore white gloves. Yes, I said white gloves. It sounds absolutely unbelievable, but in the "olden" days, we dressed up to go shopping. Mom and I donned our finest attire, pulled on our white, tight-fitting, cotton gloves, and off we went to either Meyersdale or Cumberland. To us, Cumberland was the BIG city. We might as well have been shopping on Madison Avenue in New York City. It was an exciting adventure for a little girl.

And speaking of getting "dressed up," I remember the soldiers in their uniforms and the endless procession of U.S. Army trucks, jeeps and trailers that passed through town every summer! They were all the same drab green and many had a white star painted on the door. They were National Guard troops on their way to summer training camp. As soon as I spied the first few trucks, I knew it was time for my "walk." I dashed into the house put on a cute pair of short shorts and strolled up town. The guys waved or whistled and even honked! Occasionally, I waved back, but usually I pretended to ignore them. I sure thought I was hot stuff! But I was just a little girl --- what was I thinking? I can't imagine what I would have done if one of those guys had actually hopped off the moving truck and started chasing me. I would have been horrified. But I was a skinny kid who knew how to run fast, so I could have made it safely back to Grandma's house.

I have discussed the more significant things that we did over the summer months, but this list is by no means exhaustive. My childhood memories of summertime in Grantsville include a myriad of wonderful experiences and adventures, large and small.

CHAPTER 12

CHICKENS AND EGGS

This book is entitled "Fresh Eggs" because, as previously mentioned, these were the words on a big sign in front of our home on Main Street. For many years during my childhood, Dad raised chickens and sold eggs. Although I remembered that our diet included a lot of eggs, I realized that I really didn't know very much about Dad's chicken and egg operation. I knew about his egg candling and washing machines in the basement. I also was aware of the big black barn across the alley next to the orchard and garden. However, I never went into a chicken coop, and I never helped feed the chickens or gather the eggs. I also didn't know how many chickens or what kind of chickens he raised. So, I asked my older brother, Andy, if he knew anything about Dad's chicken and egg operation. Oh boy did he! It turned out that Andy was very much engaged in helping Dad with this family enterprise.

Andy related that Dad got the baby chicks in boxes shipped through the mail each spring, and he raised the peeps in the kitchen for the first week or so. That information sure brought back some memories. I remember the excitement surrounding the arrival of the peeps. I used to hold them in my hands very carefully. They were cute fuzzy, yellow balls that moved around in the cardboard box like bumper cars and peeped continuously. We called them "pee-pees."

According to Andy, Dad kept his egg laying flock in that large black barn behind our house, where there were about 300 chickens. Although I used to play around this building, I never knew there were chickens in there. They also must have been very quiet, because I never heard them making any clucking noises. Surprisingly, Andy said that Dad also had chickens in four other buildings around the neighborhood!

The second-largest barn was up the alley behind Mr. Huff's house. Andy estimated that there were probably close to 300 chickens on the second floor. Adjacent to that barn, a smaller, flat building held a smaller flock of approximately 150 chickens. The second-floor barn area was closed off by a wire door that Dad kept closed with a piece of string. One afternoon Andy was feeding those chickens when they were startled by a loud noise in the alley. All the chickens flew into the air in a cloud of dust. Enough of them flew against the wire door to cause the string to break, and chickens poured out of the second floor and into all the trees and bushes in Mr. Huff's back yard. Andy was mortified and went to get Dad to help round them up. Dad didn't ask any questions but just smiled. Then Dad and Andy worked to get the chickens out of the trees and back into the coop.

The third area was a pair of buildings behind the Casselman Inn at the east end of town. There were probably 250 chickens in the large building and maybe 50 in the smaller one. Andy recalled one incident that occurred one summer. The Grantsville town fair was held at the fairgrounds across the street from Dad's chicken coops. One night gypsies from the fair broke into the smaller coop and slept there. They also ate some of the chickens!

During one cold spell, the water line froze in the larger building. Dad hired some guys to thaw it with a blowtorch. In the process, they managed to leave some sparks burning beneath the floor. During the following cold night, the building burst into flames. All the chickens were killed.

Incredible as it may seem, I was totally unaware of these events. I think I was just too little. Andy, however, was deeply involved with the Dad's chickens. Feeding and watering these birds and gathering their eggs at widely separated locations were chores for Andy every afternoon after school. He fed the chickens with a mash made from ground meal and buttermilk.

However, Andy didn't consider this the worst task associated with the chickens. In his opinion, the worst job was cutting off their upper beaks so that they wouldn't peck each other to death. He and Dad always did this procedure fairly late at night when the chickens had gone to sleep. Dad had a little debeaking machine that worked something like a big toenail clipper, except that it had a very hot bar on it. After you clipped off the upper beak, you held the stub against the hot bar to sear the wound. This caused a very bad smell.

At first, Dad cleaned, candled and graded the eggs by hand on the kitchen table every evening. Mom soon got tired of that mess. So, they purchased an egg-washing machine and a candling-grading machine that were kept in the cellar.

Dad must have spent many hours carefully weighing each delicate fresh egg, sorting them by size, and then washing and placing them into their protective cartons. These cartons were then sold to customers, either individually or in bulk. Dad had a wholesale arrangement with a local egg distributor. Running the candling-grading machine and putting the eggs into cartons for sale was Andy's favorite job. Most of the eggs were packed in cases of 30 dozen each. The chickens produced five or six cases every week.

Strangely, I never watched either of them perform these time-consuming operations, or if I did, I do not remember it. However, I recall some of the customers who used to come to the house to buy eggs. One lady, who was from the Cumberland area, was always so well dressed and so lovely to Mom. They would often talk after she purchased eggs.

In addition to eggs, we also ate a lot of chicken. Dad would bring one into the back yard hanging by its legs. He chopped the head off with a hatchet and let the body run around the yard "like a chicken with its head cut off" until it collapsed. Then he dipped it in a bucket of scalding hot water and pulled the feathers off, before removing its insides and feet. We definitely had fresh chicken for dinner at our house.

Dad's biggest chicken experiment was Henry, the Bantam rooster. Webster's dictionary defines "bantam" not only as a variety of very small chicken, but also as a "small, feisty, quarrelsome, and combative person." Both described Henry perfectly. Of course, he was not a person, but he was a small chicken who was combative and feisty. He was also pretty smart for a rooster.

Dad with Mom Holding Henry…One of His Calmer Moments

I think Dad brought Henry into our lives as a kind of pet. Henry was an extremely handsome bird with beautiful brownish red feathers that glistened in the sunlight set off by shiny black feathers that covered certain areas of his plump, little body. He had a rigid, crimson comb and beady little, yellow-iris eyes. We also had another Bantam "pet" named Henrietta, who was a great little chicken. She was beautiful also, but unlike Henry, she was totally black.

Henry soon took over the entire back yard and attacked anything that moved. He was a menace! I hated Henry with a passion, and he seemed to hate me too. I was sure that Henry waited for me every morning so that he could attack me as I ran across the lawn. As soon as I spotted him, I would break into a run and he would begin to run too. Henry always caught up with me and then pecked viciously at my ankles. My only defense was a small, black patent leather purse (I have no idea what I carried in this little bag), but I used it as a weapon to hit him over the head. I eventually made it to the garage or wherever I was going, but it was an ordeal nearly every morning. I was terrified of Henry!

Mom finally had enough when Henry attacked her while she was hanging up the laundry. I honestly don't know what became of Henry and Henrietta. I was told that Dad took both of these animals out to a local farm, and I never saw either one of them again. Andy says that Henry was served for dinner!

CHAPTER 13

ALICE IN WONDERLAND

I have written about my early years and the people who were central to my life. But how have I been affected by the "Alice in Wonderland" events that defined my childhood? Who am I today?

I wrote this memoir for my family, specifically for my son, Brendan. I wondered how well he knew me or where I came from. I was concerned that he may have information about my childhood that was incorrect or incomplete. I felt the need to get the facts down in writing; that it was important to tell Brendan about my side of the family. Ever since my divorce from Brendan's father and my subsequent move to the east coast, Brendan and I have lived apart. This breaks my heart; I have missed so much of his life. Nevertheless, I love him very much.

When he turned 30 years old on June 4, 2009, I felt compelled to complete this book. Although I started it many years earlier to tell Brendan my story, the changes going on his life increased my desire to finish it. Brendan was looking forward to getting married and starting his own family. An exciting note: On April 9, 2010, Brendan and his wife Melissa had a baby boy and named my first grandson, Antone Davis Pearson.

All things considered, I had a wonderful childhood. It is my strong, unwavering belief that growing up in Grantsville provided the solid foundation of my sound emotional well-being and happiness today. Of course, I have my moments of "unsoundness" and "unhappiness," but I am content with my life, and I have the most wonderful husband in the world. Yes, I had a few troublesome experiences as a young girl, but they too are a part of who I am today. I was always loved, well fed, and I had a roof over my head. I am a strong, healthy, intelligent, decent human being. One cannot ask for more than that.

I consider myself extremely fortunate to have grown up in a small town. Life was much simpler back then. My brothers and I felt safe running all around town and across the entire countryside. We had our whole "kids" world to enjoy. Because of my small-town upbringing, I was trusting as a child and even as a young adult. Unfortunately, my trust in the human race began to fade once I left Grantsville.

I wish I knew whether my growing cynicism and distrust of others is the cumulative affect of all of the bad things that have happened in our world over the past 60 years, or a product of my genetic blueprint. I sometimes wonder which personality traits I inherited from Dad. I am not sure how trusting he was of others either. We inherit many things from our parents, but I am not sure "trust" is a matter of genetics. Trust is more likely developed through nurture than through nature. I do not blindly trust others; their trust must be earned over time. Unfortunately, I believe that some of the negative things about me may stem from Dad's lack of affection towards me as a little girl. His legacy has been somewhat of a burden for me.

Not all of who I am can be attributed specifically to my years in Grantsville. My teenage years in Catonsville had a lasting affect on me as well. It was during that time that Dad became more worrisome and detrimental to me psychologically. However, I believe that his lack of affection towards me and his occasional drinking episodes when I was a young child did have a negative impact on me.

Although my childhood was a very happy one, my Dad's beer binges occasionally interrupted it. He wasn't drunk that often, but I hid from him on occasion. He was kind of scary to a little girl, though he never hurt me physically. He was just there, sometimes drunk. Mostly Mom had to deal with him. As kids, we were outside playing most of the time. What hurt me most about Dad was that he just never talked to me or had much to do with me at all. He never hugged me that I can remember. He never told me he loved me, although I am absolutely certain that he did love me very much.

Like Dad, I am reticent to show affection. Perhaps I fear rejection. In a way, I felt rejected by Dad, although it was not a conscious effort on his part. Also like Dad, I am not very forgiving of others, particularly people I do not know who are rude or nasty to me. According to Mom, Dad sometimes just disliked a person for no good reason. I am different that way --- a person must show me a reason before I will dislike them. Once crossed, however, I rarely "turn the other cheek." I am not sure why. Perhaps it is because I have been through so much in my life (not just Dad stuff) that I don't want to waste my time, energy, and especially my affection on people who are mean-spirited, pseudo-intellectuals, dangerous, manipulative, or who spread false rumors or create hard feelings. At this point in my life, I prefer to be around people who are gentle, open, honest, and kind, and who genuinely care about me as a person.

In addition, I do not let anyone get to know me easily. It takes me a long time to build a relationship with someone. I can be quite guarded around people and not allow the true me to shine. I don't allow many people to observe my "goofy" and talkative side. Perhaps I should. Here again, I think that this is a product of fear of rejection.

Because of the occasionally tense environment in my home, mostly during my teen years, I do not deal well with big changes in my life. I prefer things to be quiet and stable. I remember Dad being upset with Mom whenever she accidentally made a loud noise in the kitchen. I hate sudden, loud noises, too! I also dislike loud music, noisy commercials on the television, and people eating popcorn next to me in a movie theater!

My last big "wart," at least that I am willing to reveal, is that I tend to be a bit neurotic. I say this because sometimes I will become obsessed about something (like getting this book written)! I also worry way too much about dumb, unimportant things. I am compulsive about cleaning the house for company or before taking a long trip. I am terrified of getting lost when I am driving, I hate to loose stuff, and it makes me crazy when someone does not believe me. Did I inherit the tendency to worry from Dad?

I am fortunate to be married to a fantastic man who truly understands me and loves me for who I am --- "warts" and all. He knows that I don't deal with change well. When it comes along, as it inevitably must, he lets me rant and rave until I get over the angst, at which point I am gung ho for the change, even a big change. David Trauger is someone I need to be around. He is extraordinarily kind, intelligent, open and honest. He genuinely cares for me and about me. What you see is what you get with David. He has no hidden "weird" side to his strikingly calm personality. How I finally got so lucky, I will never know. I love him very much.

Mom was the perfect counter balance to Dad. I am so fortunate to have had her in my life. As I have mentioned earlier, she had an inner core of strength that fortified all who knew her, including me. She was always there for me and for all of her children, for that matter. Unlike Dad, Mom was very affectionate. I only wish she had been more so to me as a young child. It is my belief, however, that she was so busy keeping Dad out of trouble, coping with his occasional bouts of beer drinking, doing housework, cooking, going to school or work, and keeping our collective heads "above water," that she had little time and energy left to give us a hug. But she did absolutely all she could in the "show of affection" category. I knew that she loved me --- it always showed in everything she did, from hiding Easter egg baskets to making me hot cocoa and buttered toast late at night. Because of Mom's love for me, I am a better person.

Everyone described in this book was or is a person of great warmth, caring, integrity, and intelligence. Dad had most of these qualities too, to some degree during different stages in his life. He was highly intelligent, and I know that he always cared for me. But he was plagued by demons throughout his entire life. Dad was never able to be the open, warm, caring father that I needed or desired. It was only at the end of his life when he was gravely ill, that I witnessed a gentle "Dad" spark. He was troubled, but I loved him nonetheless.

One final comment concerning Dad: when I began this book, I was somewhat angry with him for not always being there for me. But, in the process of writing as well as delving into the Faith and Davis genealogies, I have come to see Dad very differently. Considering his humble beginnings and his birth into such an enormous family --- a family which no doubt, struggled every day to survive --- Dad succeeded in carving out a pretty good life for him and his family. To his credit, he obtained a good education, putting himself through college. He married a great lady and stayed married for over 50 years!!! He provided a generous income and comfortable lifestyle for his family as a dedicated teacher. I never knew Dad to miss one day of teaching --- a profession which he loved.

POSTSCRIPT

I feel very fortunate to have grown up in the small town of Grantsville. This town, located in rural western Maryland, created the idyllic setting for me to have a wonderful childhood. My memories were so strong that I wanted to write this book to share with my son and his family.

After attending grade school in Grantsville and junior high school at Northern High School, our family moved to Catonsville in Baltimore County, Maryland. My small town life came to an abrupt end there. Nevertheless, I enjoyed my time in Catonsville and I graduated from Catonsville High School in 1967.

Shortly after graduation, I was recruited by the National Security Agency (NSA) located at Fort Meade in Prince George's County. I passed the necessary tests and began working for NSA in August 1967. In 1974, I applied for an administrative position in Frankfurt, Germany. I was accepted for the position and moved all of my worldly possessions, including a bright yellow Pontiac Firebird, to Germany. I vividly remember Mom asking me "Are you sure you want to do this?" I said "Yes!" And off I flew to Frankfurt where I stayed until 1977.

My position in Germany was with the NSA Engineering Division. I greatly enjoyed this assignment, and I was able to visit most of the countries in western Europe. I would have stayed longer, but I met a young U.S. Army Captain, David W. Pearson, whom I subsequently married in December 1977 in Paducah, Kentucky. On June 4, 1979, I gave birth to my only son, Brendan Davis Pearson.

During my time in Paducah, I worked as a secretary for the Federal Aviation Administration (FAA) at the Flight Service Station. In January 1979, Muhammad Ali, stopped over briefly on his way to Louisville. I was very pregnant at the time, but I went to the cafeteria with a group of people to see him. For some reason, Ali noticed me and summoned me. It was a treat for me to meet him and I was able to get his autograph.

In 1980, David and I left Kentucky and moved to Minnesota, Pearson's home state. There I worked briefly for the Social Security Administration in Minneapolis. David Pearson and I divorced in February 1983.

After I left the Social Security Administration, I began working as a secretary in the Refuges and Wildlife Division for the U.S. Fish and Wildlife Service (FWS), which was located at Fort Snelling in the Twin Cities. I worked in various positions in the Regional Office from 1984 to 1987. During that time, I met Dr. David Lee Trauger who, at the time, was the Director of the Patuxent Wildlife Research Center located in Laurel, Maryland. He was visiting the FWS office in the Twin Cities, where a colleague introduced David to me.

Long story short, David and I dated for about a year and developed a long distance relationship. After a marriage proposal on "Going to the

Sun Highway" in Glacier National Park, Montana, David moved me along with, once again, "all of my worldly possessions" to Arlington, Virginia. We were married at the Morrison House in Alexandria, Virginia, on June 29, 1988.

My colleagues at the FWS arranged a job transfer to the Washington Office, where I worked with the Division of Realty and then the Division of Refuges. I always wanted to complete my college education, and I had accumulated a number of credits attending classes over the years. However, David and I decided that if I was ever going to complete my degree during my lifetime that I needed to be a full-time student. Therefore, in 1989, I left the Federal Government to enroll at George Mason University located in Fairfax, Virginia. I received my Bachelor's Degree in Social Work in May 1993. While earning this degree, I worked with the elderly, the mentally and physically disabled, and young people with emotional problems. All of these populations were challenging but very rewarding.

Shortly after graduation from George Mason University, I began to work again for the Federal Government --- this time with the U.S. Geological Survey (USGS) in Reston, Virginia. My first position was in the Division of Procurement, where I essentially performed administrative duties. Then I applied for a USGS position as "Personnel Management Specialist" for which I was hired in the Office of Human Resources. I was selected for this coveted position for a number of important reasons, but one of the main reasons was my high academic achievement at George Mason University.

I worked as a Personnel Management Specialist, where I was involved in a diversity of interesting assignments. One of my accomplishments was the development of vocational brochures for all of the scientific disciplines employed by USGS. These documents were used for recruitment purposes throughout the United States. In August 1999, I retired from the U.S. Government with nearly 30 years of public service.

In 2002, David and I moved back to the land that I loved – Mountain Maryland. We bought a home on Dan's Mountain near Frostburg, Maryland. In 2003, I attended a meeting of local business leaders in Grantsville. At that meeting, I met the Mayor of Grantsville, who invited me to help establish a museum for Grantsville. Subsequently, I volunteered to take on this challenging project, and I was named the unpaid Curator of the yet to be established Grantsville Community Museum.

With the help of David, I began from the ground up creating this new museum in the old First State Bank building on Main Street. Over the next year, I did everything --- selecting new flooring, supervising building renovations, procuring display cases, gathering historical items from the local area, organizing fundraisers, writing grant proposals, attending museum workshops, learning curatorial protocols, developing displays of artifacts, and accomplishing a myriad of other tasks. It was truly a labor of love.

Alice at the Grantsville Community Museum

The Grantsville Community Museum opened in May 2005. In time, I handed over the Museum to two women who had lived in Grantsville most of their lives. The Museum continues to create interest and pride in the community, as well as to attract visitors from near and far. I experienced great joy in establishing the Museum as a personal legacy for the town that I so loved as a child.

Recently, I have been working with my older brother, Andy, and David on my family genealogy. I am investigating both the Davis and the Faith families. This has been an interesting and exciting time, as I gained a deeper understanding of my family roots. I also reconnected with some family members with whom I had not been in touch for many years, and I also met several relatives that I never knew existed. I have learned a great deal about both sides of my family, and I have visited many of the locations where my forebears lived. Another major benefit is that working together with Andy has brought us closer together. This was important not only to me, but I also wanted my son, Brendan to know about his roots and learn about his ancestors.

ABOUT THE AUTHOR

Alice L. Faith-Trauger wrote this memoir about growing up in western Maryland. After retirement from public service, she helped establish the Grantsville Community Museum as a personal legacy to the small town that was instrumental during her formative years. The museum continues to create interest and pride in the community.